75 FLORAL BLOCKS
TO KNIT

75 FLORAL BLOCKS
TO KNIT

Beautiful Patterns to Mix & Match for
Afghans, Throws, Baby Blankets, & More

LESLEY STANFIELD

St. Martin's Griffin
New York

75 FLORAL BLOCKS TO KNIT

Copyright © 2013 Quarto, Inc. All rights reserved.
Printed in China. For information, address St. Martin's Press,
175 Fifth Avenue, New York, N.Y. 10010.

www.stmartins.com

Library of Congress Cataloging-in-Publication Data
Available Upon Request

ISBN: 978-1-250-01902-8

First U.S. Edition: January 2013

10 9 8 7 6 5 4 3 2 1

Conceived, designed, and produced by
Quarto Publishing plc
The Old Brewery
6 Blundell Street
London N7 9BH

QUAR: FKBL

Project Editor: Victoria Lyle
Pattern Checker: Susan Horan
Illustrator: Kuo Kang Chen
Photographer (directory): Philip Wilkins
Photographer (projects): Nicki Dowey
Proofreader: Ruth Patrick
Indexer: Helen Snaith
Art Director: Caroline Guest
Creative Director: Moira Clinch
Publisher: Paul Carslake

Color separation by Pica Digital Pte Ltd, Singapore
Printed by 1010 Printing International Ltd, China

CONTENTS

FOREWORD

From stylized to naturalistic, these botanical images offer a kaleidoscope of ideas for adventurous knitters.

Many of the blocks require quite basic skills, while others are more complicated but really only need a little patience. They all offer a great variety of techniques from stitch patterns to color work.

The beauty of making single units like these is that the knitting is very portable and most can be completed quite quickly. The blocks can be used for patchwork or they can stand alone, as suggested in the projects section.

Do treat these designs as a starting point to free your imagination, to mix your own palette, and to create flower arrangements with your needles.

LESLEY STANFIELD

ABOUT THIS BOOK

This book provides a delightful collection of 75 floral blocks to knit. Each is both charming in its own right and looks fantastic when worked with others to create baby blankets, accessories, home furnishings, or other projects of your own devising.

DIRECTORY
(pages 8–15)

The block selector displays all 75 designs in miniature together. Flick through this colorful visual guide for inspiration, select your design, and then turn to the relevant page of instructions to create your chosen piece.

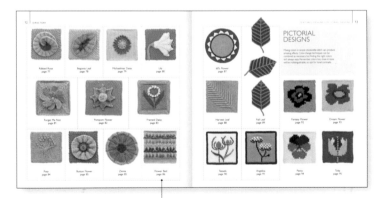

Each block is labeled with a number that corresponds to the relevant pattern in the Instructions chapter.

CHAPTER 1: USEFUL TECHNIQUES
(pages 16–33)

This chapter covers basics such as equipment, yarn, and abbreviations. It also includes information on the techniques used in the book, as well as how to work edgings and join blocks.

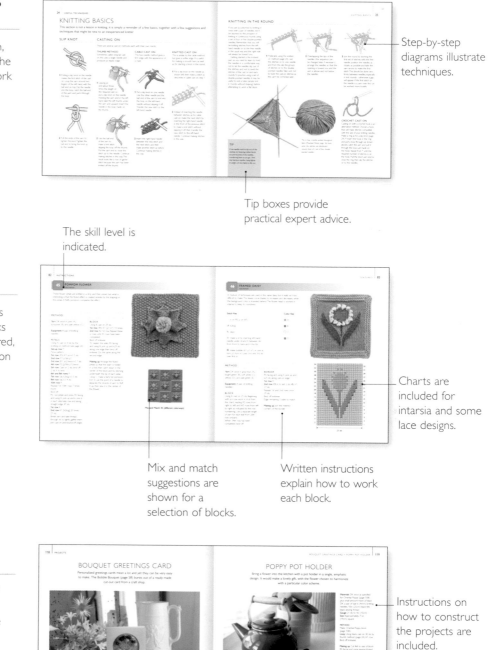

Step-by-step diagrams illustrate techniques.

Tip boxes provide practical expert advice.

The skill level is indicated.

CHAPTER 2: INSTRUCTIONS
(pages 34–111)

In this chapter you'll find written patterns as well as charts for intarsia and some lace designs. The blocks are organized into three sections: traditional, textured, and pictorial. The traditional section draws inspiration from old, lacy, floral knitting patterns, the textured section includes bobbles, loops, picots, and other textured stitches, and the pictorial section features some beautiful intarsia designs.

Charts are included for intarsia and some lace designs.

Mix and match suggestions are shown for a selection of blocks.

Written instructions explain how to work each block.

CHAPTER 3: PROJECTS
(pages 112–125)

The blocks in this book can be used in a myriad of ways. This chapter presents a selection of stunning designs to inspire you with ideas of how to use the blocks in your own projects.

Instructions on how to construct the projects are included.

Each project is illustrated with a photograph of the finished item.

TRADITIONAL DESIGNS

Some of these designs are taken from quilts of the nineteenth century when they would have been worked in white cotton. Others are adaptations of old designs, brought up to date with simplification and the use of color.

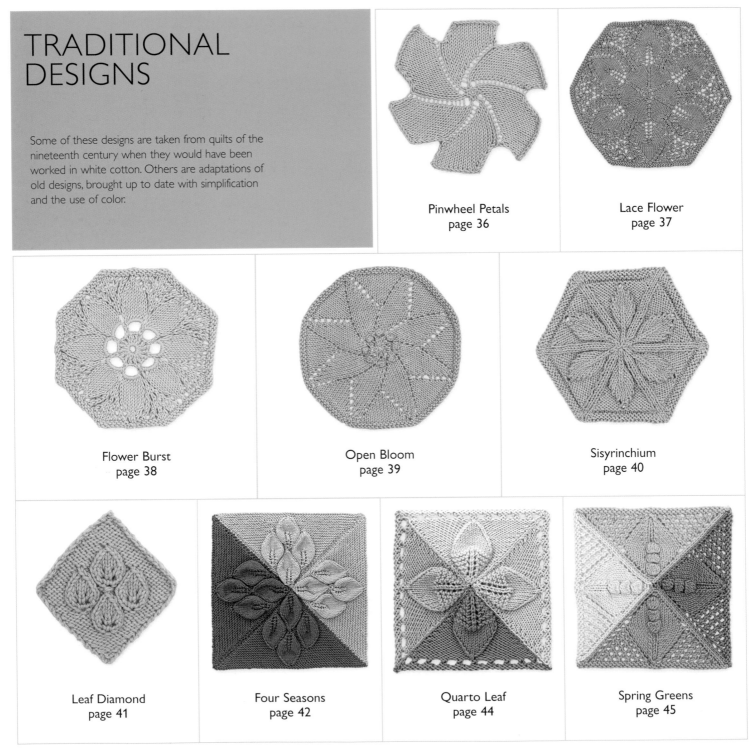

Pinwheel Petals
page 36

Lace Flower
page 37

Flower Burst
page 38

Open Bloom
page 39

Sisyrinchium
page 40

Leaf Diamond
page 41

Four Seasons
page 42

Quarto Leaf
page 44

Spring Greens
page 45

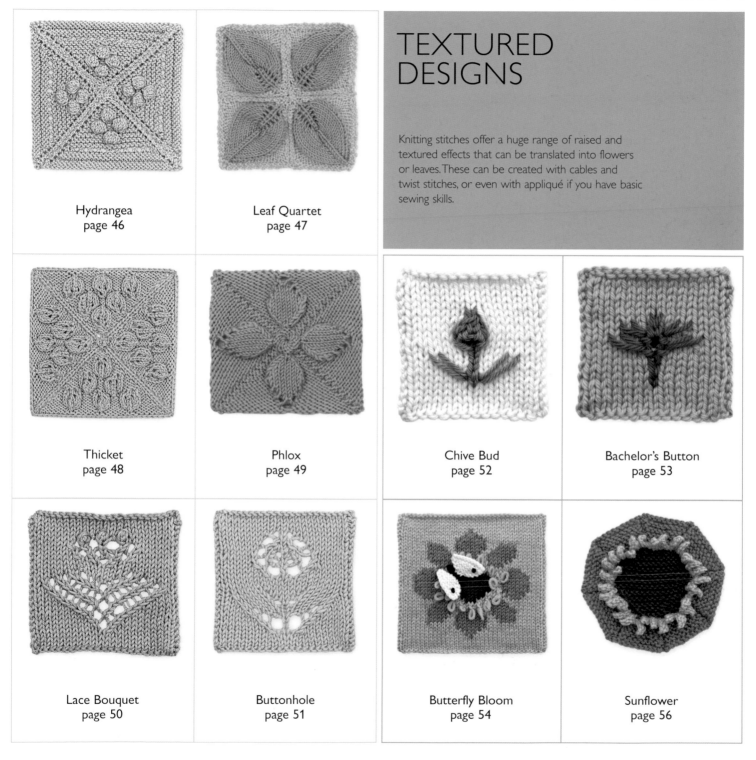

TEXTURED DESIGNS

Knitting stitches offer a huge range of raised and textured effects that can be translated into flowers or leaves. These can be created with cables and twist stitches, or even with appliqué if you have basic sewing skills.

Hydrangea
page 46

Leaf Quartet
page 47

Thicket
page 48

Phlox
page 49

Chive Bud
page 52

Bachelor's Button
page 53

Lace Bouquet
page 50

Buttonhole
page 51

Butterfly Bloom
page 54

Sunflower
page 56

Star Flower
page 57

Bobble Bouquet
page 58

70's Daisy
page 59

Poppy
page 60

Crocus
page 61

Formal Flower
page 62

Spring Bulb
page 63

Cord Flower
page 64

Cord Leaf
page 65

Maple Leaf
page 66

Clematis
page 67

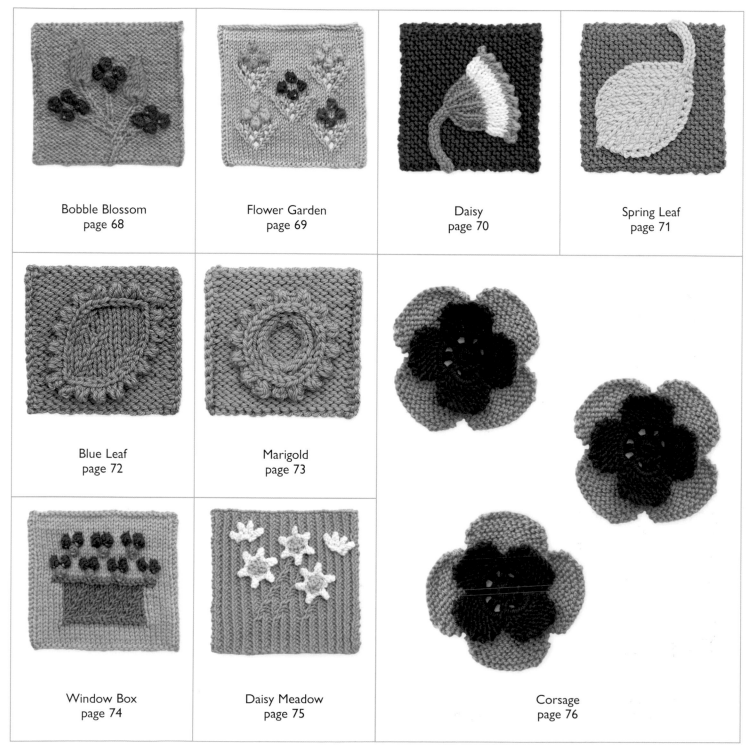

Bobble Blossom
page 68

Flower Garden
page 69

Daisy
page 70

Spring Leaf
page 71

Blue Leaf
page 72

Marigold
page 73

Window Box
page 74

Daisy Meadow
page 75

Corsage
page 76

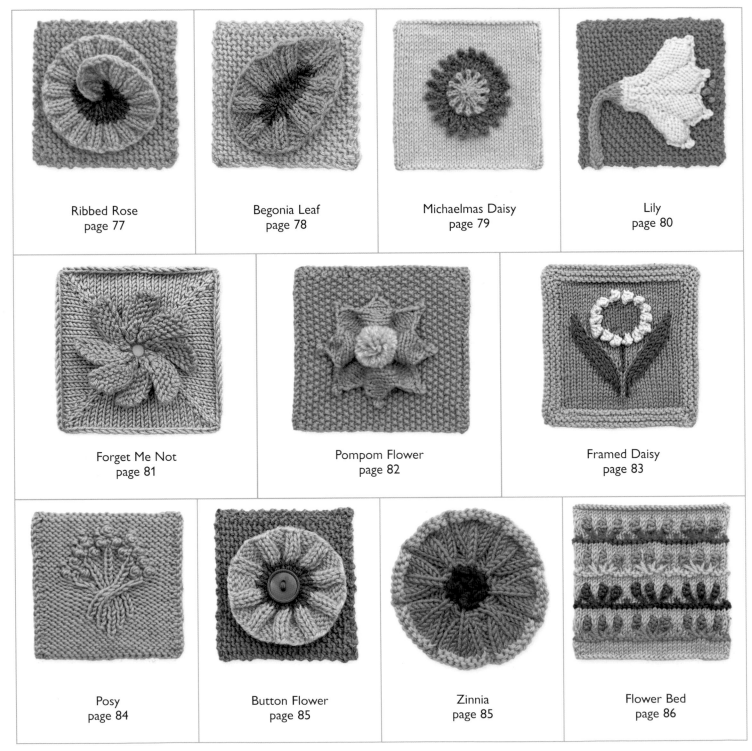

Ribbed Rose
page 77

Begonia Leaf
page 78

Michaelmas Daisy
page 79

Lily
page 80

Forget Me Not
page 81

Pompom Flower
page 82

Framed Daisy
page 83

Posy
page 84

Button Flower
page 85

Zinnia
page 85

Flower Bed
page 86

PICTORIAL DESIGNS

Mixing colors in simple stockinette stitch can produce amazing effects. Color-change techniques can be combined as necessary, but finding the right colors isn't always easy. Remember, colors too close in tone will be indistinguishable, so opt for tonal contrasts.

60's Flower
page 87

Fall Leaf
page 89

Harvest Leaf
page 88

Fantasy Flower
page 92

Dream Flower
page 93

Teasels
page 90

Angelica
page 91

Pansy
page 94

Tulip
page 95

Mock Orange
page 96

Snowdrop
page 97

Fig Leaf
page 102

Thistle
page 98

Fritillary
page 99

Oak Leaf
page 103

Rose Bud
page 100

Rose
page 101

Rowan Leaf
page 104

Lime Leaf
page 105

Tulip Tree Leaf
page 106

Cheese Plant Leaf
page 107

Oriental Poppy
page 108

Iris
page 109

Amaryllis
page 110

Gerbera
page 111

1

USEFUL TECHNIQUES

This chapter covers basics such as equipment, yarn, and abbreviations. It also includes information on the techniques used in the book, as well as how to work edgings and join blocks.

EQUIPMENT

The basic tools for knitting are simple, portable, and relatively inexpensive.

KNITTING NEEDLES

Few needle sizes are specified in this book, so you will want to vary your choice of needle depending on the yarn you are using. Pairs of knitting needles are made in a variety of lengths and the length you prefer will depend on the way you hold the needles. For most of the designs in this book, a conventional pair of needles is used, but two double-pointed needles are needed to make a cord, and four or sometimes five double-pointed needles are needed where there is knitting in the round.

Wood or bamboo needles are lightweight and some knitters find them less tiring to the hands than metal. They are also useful for knitting with smooth yarns because there is less tendency for them to slip out of the stitches.

Double-pointed needles are sold in sets of four or five in most of the same sizes as pairs of needles.

Cable needles (short, double-pointed needles used to transfer groups of stitches) may slip out of the stitches if you knit loosely, so look for those with a curve in the middle.

Metal needles may be either steel or aluminum. These strong, smooth materials are particularly suited to speedy knitting for anyone who likes their needles to be completely rigid.

EQUIVALENT NEEDLE SIZES

Choosing the correct size of needle is crucial to obtaining a good fabric, so try to build up a collection so that you can easily substitute one size for another. Needles are sized in the US from 0 to about 20 and in Europe from 2mm to 15mm. There is not always an exact match between the two systems.

US	Europe
0	2 mm
1	2.25 mm
2	2.75 mm
3	3 mm
4	3.25 mm
5	3.5 mm
6	4 mm
7	4.5 mm
8	5 mm
9	5.5 mm
10	6 mm
10.5	6.5 or 7 mm
11	8 mm
13	9 mm
15	10 mm
17	12 or 13 mm
20	15 mm

ADDITIONAL EQUIPMENT

TAPE MEASURE

Preferably choose a tape measure that features both inches and centimeters on the same side, to familiarize yourself with both systems of measurement.

MARKERS

Readymade markers can be used to indicate a repeat or to help count stitches. Alternatively, use contrast yarn for soft, flexible markers (see page 27 for methods).

ROW COUNTER

A row counter may help you to keep track of the rows or rounds you have worked, but counting rows is easy if you remember to include the stitches on the needle as a row. Also remember that in garter stitch each ridge on the right side represents two rows.

CROCHET HOOKS

Like knitting needles, crochet hooks are readily available in metal. They usually have a flange where they are to be held. Some newer hooks are made with a soft-grip handle.

SCISSORS

Choose a small, sharp-pointed pair of scissors to cut yarn and trim ends neatly.

PINS

Long, large-headed pins are the best to use when measuring your gauge because the large colored heads won't get lost between the stitches. Old-fashioned hair pins are best for holding pieces of knitting together for sewing up; insert them at a right angle to the edge.

WOOL NEEDLES

For sewing seams, darning in yarn ends, and for duplicate stitch (see page 30) you need a blunt-tipped needle with a large eye. These are available in several sizes to suit different yarn types. They are sometimes called tapestry needles and are designed to not split the yarn.

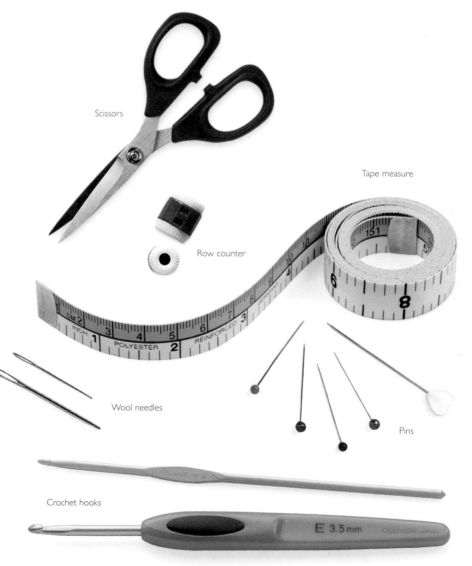

Scissors

Row counter

Tape measure

Wool needles

Pins

Crochet hooks

E 3.5 mm

TIP

If you find it tiring to use a conventional crochet hook, especially in a small size, you can push a cork onto the hook to improvise a soft-grip handle.

YARN CHOICE

There are abundant yarn types and colors to choose from. Changing the type of yarn will produce a different result and scale, so it can be very rewarding to experiment.

YARNS

Yarns are available in a range of weights, from lace weight to super bulky. Because yarns may vary from one manufacturer to another and certainly change from one fiber to another, generic yarn types are mostly used in this book. You should be aware of the characteristics of different fibers, however, from the fullness of cotton to the elasticity of wool. Because the construction of a yarn will affect its behavior, this will also influence the end result. Try using as many different yarns as possible until you are confident.

If you really want to create a florist's shop, separate your yarns into color groups and keep these in transparent plastic containers so that you have a palette of colors to work with. Don't limit yourself to knitting yarns and look out for interesting colors among embroidery wools.

READING BALL BANDS

Most yarns have bands that give you the information you need to make the right choice for any project, for example, details about fiber content, recommended needle size, length of yarn on each ball, and washing instructions.

Color

22004

Dyelot

2 8 8

If purchasing more than one ball of the same color, make sure dye-lot numbers match because any slight difference may become visible once the yarn is knitted up.

Debbie Bliss

Rialto 4ply

100% Merino wool extrafine superwash
Made in Italy

Ball length and weight. Some fibers are heavier than others so, for example, 2oz (50g) of cotton yarn may well be shorter in length than 2oz (50g) of woolen yarn with a similar recommended gauge.

180m / 50g
198 yds / 50g

Recommended needle size for stockinette stitch.

US 3
3.25mm

Tension
10 x10cm sq
36 rows
28 sts

Gauge guide gives the recommended gauge for the yarn (see page 21).

Distributed by
Designer Yarns Limited

www.designeryarns.uk.com

TIP

Care instructions are usually provided as symbols that tell you if the yarn can be hand- or machine-washed, dry-cleaned, pressed, and so on. Keep a ball band from each project for future reference, and if the item is a gift, make sure you pass on the details.

FABRIC

I think that, when knitting blocks, the fabric is usually more critical than the size, so use a yarn and needle size that are compatible for your project. For example, a firm fabric would be suitable for a bag, whereas a scarf would need to be soft and supple.

Obviously, using a finer yarn will produce a daintier result and a thicker yarn will produce something chunkier. For example, the 60's Flower (page 87) made with sport weight measures approximately 8in (20cm) in diameter, whereas the same design in worsted weight (the retro cushion on pages 116–117) measures approximately 14in (34cm) across.

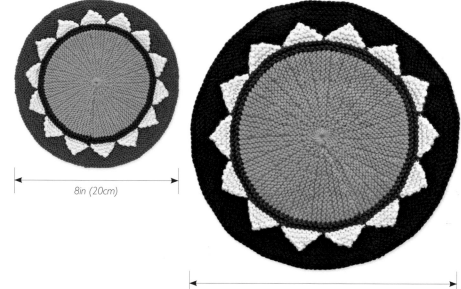

8in (20cm)

14in (34cm)

CALCULATING SIZE

If it is important to know the finished size of your block, some preparatory calculations will need to be made.

Gauge is the key to size in knitting and the starting point is usually the information given on the ball band, which states a recommended stitch and row count to 4in (10cm) over stockinette stitch. So, for example, if the stitch gauge is 22 sts to 4in (10cm), divide the number of stitches in your square block by 22 and multiply by 4 (10) to calculate the width. Similarly, if the row gauge is 28 rows to 4in (10cm), divide the number of rows in your block by 28 and multiply by 4 (10) to calculate the depth.

Note that stranded knitting, garter stitch, and seed stitch will all differ in gauge from stockinette stitch.

Estimating the size of a block knitted in the round is trickier. If the block is round, you could take the number of stitches at the outside edge and use a stitch calculation like the one above to give the approximate circumference.

Similarly, the outside edges of a hexagon or octagon could be estimated by taking the gauge along one edge and multiplying it by 6 or 8, as appropriate.

The row gauge would give, very roughly, the depth of the rounds from center to outside edge.

MEASURING GAUGE

To see if you are matching the gauge given on a ball band, or to measure the gauge of a swatch made in your chosen needle size and yarn, follow these instructions.

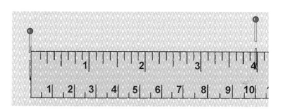

1 Lay the swatch on a flat surface. Using a ruler or tape measure, place two pins exactly 4in (10cm) apart at the center of the swatch as shown. Count the number of stitches (including any half stitches) along a straight row between the pins.

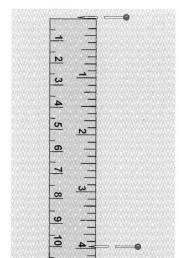

2 Now place the pins 4in (10cm) apart vertically and count the number of rows between them along a straight line of stitches.

ABBREVIATIONS AND CHARTS

All the symbols used in the charts are shown and explained on the relevant pages. However, information and tips on reading charts are included here. All the abbreviations used in the book are also listed for easy reference.

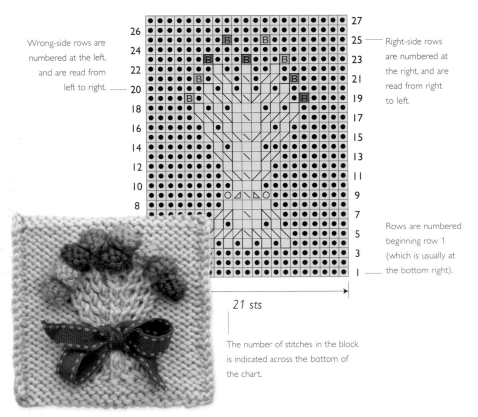

Wrong-side rows are numbered at the left, and are read from left to right.

Right-side rows are numbered at the right, and are read from right to left.

Rows are numbered beginning row 1 (which is usually at the bottom right).

21 sts

The number of stitches in the block is indicated across the bottom of the chart.

READING CHARTS

Charts are a visual representation of how to work a pattern; the symbols are used to create a stylized picture. It is usually easier to find your place in a chart than in a lengthy set of instructions.

Reading order

Each chart should be read from the lower edge upward, progressing in the same way as the work, with each row of squares on the chart representing a row of knitting. All right-side rows are read from right to left, and all wrong-side rows are read from left to right. The rows are numbered, and in most cases the first and odd-numbered rows are right-side rows, starting on the right.

Before you start

Read through your chosen chart before starting to knit to make sure that you understand how to work the symbols used to create the stitch pattern. Check also for any other requirements.

Supplementary charts

A chart may have separate supplementary charts, for instance, to show leaves (see page 68). The row numbers on the supplementary chart correspond to the numbers outlined on the main chart, and each row should be worked in the position indicated.

Color knitting

Color charts in stockinette stitch are read in the same way as stitch pattern charts with every right-side row knit and every wrong-side row purl, using colors as shown.

TIPS TO MAKE THE CHARTS WORK FOR YOU

- When working from a chart, you may find it easier to cover up the rows above the one you're working, both to mark your place and to see how the stitches relate to the rows below without worrying about what comes next.
- Photocopies are very useful. An enlarged photocopy of your chosen chart makes it easier to carry about and use anywhere.

- Cross through rows or repeats as you work on the photocopy. This will aid you while you work without spoiling the copy in the book.

KNITTING ABBREVIATIONS

c2b   slip one stitch onto cable needle and hold at back, k1 then k1 from cable needle

c2bp   slip one stitch onto cable needle and hold at back, k1 then p1 from cable needle

c2f   slip one stitch onto cable needle and hold at front, k1 then k1 from cable needle

c2fp   slip one stitch onto cable needle and hold at front, p1 then k1 from cable needle

g-st   garter stitch

k   knit

kfb   knit in front and back of stitch to make two stitches from one

k2sso   knit two together, slip stitch just made on to left-hand needle, pass next stitch over it, slip stitch back on to right-hand needle

m1   make a stitch by lifting strand between stitches from the front and knit in back of strand

m1L   as m1, noting that new stitch slants to the left

m1R   make a stitch by lifting strand between stitches from the back and knit in front of strand to make a stitch that slants to the right

p   purl

pfb   purl in front and back of stitch to make two stitches from one

RS   right side(s)

skpo   slip one stitch knitwise, knit one, pass slipped st over (this, like ssk below, is a method of making a single decrease that slants to the left)

s2kpo   slip two stitches as if to knit two together, knit one, pass the slipped stitches over

sk2po   slip one stitch knitwise, knit two together, pass slipped stitch over

ssk   slip two stitches one at a time knitwise, insert point of left-hand needle into the fronts of these two stitches and knit them together (this is an alternative to skpo above)

st(s)   stitch(es)

st-st   stockinette stitch

tbl   through the back of the loop(s)

tog   together

t2L   knit in back of second stitch, then knit in front of first stitch, slip both stitches off left-hand needle together

t2R   knit in front of second stitch, then knit in back of first stitch, slip both stitches off left-hand needle together

wyab   with yarn at back

wyif   with yarn in front

WS   wrong side

yo   yarn forward and over needle to make a stitch

CROCHET ABBREVIATIONS

ch   chain

ch sp   chain space

dc   double crochet

sc   single crochet

ss   slip stitch

yrh   yarn round hook

INSTRUCTIONS

[ ]   work instructions in square brackets the number of times stated

( )   round brackets indicate a group of stitches to be worked in one place

*   an asterisk marks the point from which a section of instructions is to be repeated

KNITTING BASICS

This section is not a lesson in knitting; it is simply a reminder of a few basics, together with a few suggestions and techniques that might be new to an inexperienced knitter.

SLIP KNOT

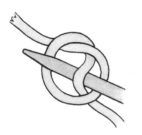

1 Putting a slip knot on the needle makes the first stitch of the cast-on. Loop the yarn around two fingers of the left hand, with the ball end on top. Dip the needle into the loop, catch the ball end of the yarn, and pull it through the loop.

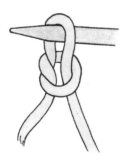

2 Pull the ends of the yarn to tighten the knot. Tighten the ball end to bring the knot up to the needle.

CASTING ON

There are several cast-on methods, each with its own merits.

THUMB METHOD
Sometimes called long-tail cast on, this uses a single needle and produces an elastic edge.

1 Leaving an end about three times the length of the required cast on, put a slip knot on the needle. Holding the yarn end in the left hand, take the left thumb under the yarn and upward. Insert the needle in the loop made on the thumb.

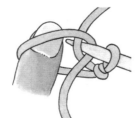

2 Use the ball end of the yarn to make a knit stitch, slipping the loop off the thumb. Pull the yarn end to close the stitch up to the needle. Continue making stitches in this way. The result looks like a row of garter stitch because the yarn has been knitted off the thumb.

CABLE CAST ON
This two-needle method gives a firm edge with the appearance of a rope.

1 Put a slip knot on one needle. Use the other needle and the ball end of the yarn to knit into the loop on the left-hand needle without slipping it off. Transfer the new stitch to the left-hand needle.

2 Insert the right-hand needle between the new stitch and the next stitch, and then make another stitch as before. Continue making stitches in this way.

KNITTED CAST ON
This is similar to the cable method, but gives a softer edge. It is useful for making a smooth hem, as well as for starting a block in the round.

1 Put a slip knot on the needle as shown left, then make a stitch as described in cable cast on, step 1.

2 Instead of inserting the needle between stitches, as for cable cast on, make the next stitch by inserting the right-hand needle in the front of the previous stitch to make a knit stitch without slipping it off, then transfer the new stitch to the left-hand needle. Continue making stitches in this way.

KNITTING IN THE ROUND

If you are accustomed to knitting in rows with a pair of needles, don't be daunted by the prospect of knitting in continuous rounds using a set of four or five double-pointed needles. Remember that you will be knitting stitches from the left-hand needle on to the free needle in the usual way, and the right side will always be toward you.

Getting started is the trickiest part, as you need to learn to hold the needles in a comfortable way, not to let the needles slip out of the stitches, and not to twist the stitches of the cast on and early rounds. To practice using a set of double-pointed needles it may be useful to knit a tube (simply knit in rounds without shaping) before attempting to work a flat block.

1 Preferably using the knitted-on method (page 24), cast the stitches on to one needle, and from this slip the groups of stitches on to the double-pointed needles. Take care not to twist the cast-on stitches as this can't be corrected later.

2 Overlapping the tips of the needles (the sequence can be changed later if necessary), arrange the needles so that the opening is toward you and the yarn is above and not below the needles.

3 Join the round by working the first set of stitches with the free needle: position the needles as closely as possible and take the yarn across to make the first stitch. This should be done very firmly between needles, especially in knit rounds—otherwise a gap will appear. If the first stitch on the needle is a yarn over, this can be worked more loosely.

This is how a partly worked hexagonal block (Pinwheel Petals, page 36) looks when the stitches are distributed around three of a set of four double-pointed needles.

CROCHET CAST ON

Casting on with a crochet hook is an alternative method. Choose a hook that will make stitches compatible with the size of your knitting needles. Make a ring as for a slip knot (page 24). * Insert the hook in the ring and pull a loop through (as shown above), catch the yarn and pull it through the loop just made on the hook; repeat from * until the required number of stitches is on the hook. Pull the short yarn end to close the ring, then slip the stitches on to the needles.

TIP

If the needles tend to slip out of the stitches, try fastening rubber bands around the ends of the needles, transferring them as you go. I find that bamboo needles, being lighter in weight, are less liable to slip out.

COLOR KNITTING

There are two methods of changing color in the row, although both can be used in one design where this is appropriate.

STRANDING

If the color not in use is to be used again after a few stitches (say, up to six stitches), it can be carried across the wrong side. Avoid taking the yarn across too tightly by spreading the stitches on the right-hand needle.

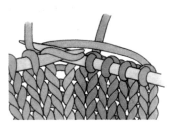

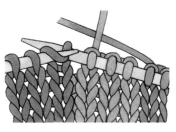

1 On knit (right-side) rows, knit the first group of stitches in the first color, then let the yarn drop. Bring the new color over the top of the dropped yarn and knit to the next group on the chart in the first color.

2 Let the second yarn drop, bring the first color under the dropped yarn and knit to the next group in the second color.

3 On purl (wrong-side) rows, purl the first group of stitches in the first color, then let the yarn drop. Bring the new color over the top of the dropped yarn and purl to the next group on the chart in the first color.

4 Let the second yarn drop, bring the first color under the dropped yarn, and purl to the next group in the second color.

INTARSIA

For color changes between larger groups of stitches it is better to use a separate length of yarn for each block of color and cross the yarns firmly at each change in order to lock the stitches together. If only two lengths of one color are needed pull the end out of the center of the ball and use both the inside and outside ends of yarn. Don't worry too much about tangling when using a lot of colors—gently pull each end out of the snarl as you need it, then, leaving not too short an end, cut and remove it when it's finished with.

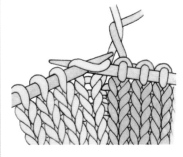

1 To change color on a knit (right-side) row, drop the first color. Pick up the second color from beneath the first color and knit along the row to the next color change.

2 To change color on a purl (wrong-side) row, drop the first color. Pick up the second color from beneath the first color and purl along the row to the next color change.

The Fig Leaf block (page 102) uses both stranding and intarsia techniques.

CORD

A very useful round cord can be made using two double-pointed needles.
Cast on 3 (or required number of) stitches and knit one row in the usual way.

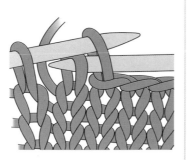

* Without turning, slide the stitches to the opposite end of the needle. Take the yarn firmly across the wrong side from left to right and knit one row. Repeat from * for the required length.

YARN MARKERS

MARKERS FOR ROWS

If markers are needed to count rows or repeats, use a length of contrast thread. * Lay it between stitches from front to back, make a stitch, and then bring it from back to front of the work. Repeat from * once. It can be pulled out when it is no longer needed.

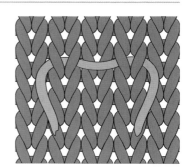

MARKERS FOR ROUNDS

Tying a tag of contrast yarn at the beginning of occasional rounds should be enough to remind you where you are in the pattern. The tags are completely flexible and can be snipped away later.

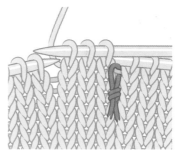

BINDING OFF

CHAIN BIND OFF

A simple knit-stitch bind off is used in most of the blocks and projects. Knit two stitches. * With the left-hand needle, lift the first stitch over the second. Knit the next stitch. Repeat from * until one stitch remains. Break the yarn, take the end through this stitch, and tighten.

A picot bind-off has been used to create petals in some of the designs in this book. This is simply a matter of casting on several stitches before binding off these and one or two more stitches. The method is the same as the chain bind-off.

When a row is only partially bound off, the count of stitches to be worked usually includes the stitch already on the needle.

INVISIBLE FASTENING OFF

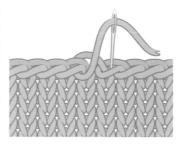

For a smooth finish to a final round, simply break the yarn and pull it through the loop of the last stitch. Thread it on to a wool needle and take it under the two top strands of the first stitch, then back into the last stitch and pull it tight until it disappears.

ENDS

The end of yarn left after casting on or binding off should be a reasonable length so that it can be used to start the sewing up or to cover up imperfections.

Joining new yarn inconspicuously is sometimes tricky. I prefer to leave both ends hanging for a little way, tension the ends to neaten the stitches either side, and then tie a neat reef knot on the wrong side, darning in the ends later.

CROCHET BASICS

Although this is a book about knitting, crochet stitches have been used at the center of a few blocks and crochet is a good way to join blocks, so the basic stitches are explained here. They are quite easy to master, so give them a go.

SLIP KNOT

 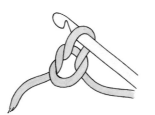

1 Putting a slip knot on the hook makes the first loop of the chain that will hold the stitches of the first row or round. Loop the yarn around two fingers of the left hand, with the ball end to the front. Insert the hook in the loop, catch the ball end of the yarn, and pull it through the loop.

2 Pull the ends of yarn to tighten the knot. Now tighten the ball end to bring the knot up to the hook and to complete the first loop, which will be the basis of the first chain.

HOOKING ACTION AND CHAIN

1 Hold the slip knot (and later the chain) between the thumb and forefinger of the left hand. Take the yarn over the second finger and under or around the little finger so that it is held taut. The right hand is then free to manipulate the hook. With a turn of the wrist, guide the tip of the hook under the yarn, catch the yarn, and pull it through the loop on the hook to make one chain. Catching the yarn is referred to as yarn round hook (abbreviation: yrh).

2 Repeat this action, drawing a new loop through the loop already on the hook until the chain is the required length. Count each v-shaped loop on the front of the chain as one chain stitch, but don't include the loop on the hook.

The Flower Burst block (page 38) has a center of crochet, with the stitches for knitting made with the hook in the third round.

NOTE

Unless the instructions state otherwise, the hook should be inserted under the two strands of yarn that form the top of the chain, or the top of the stitch. This is for stability, although the hook may be inserted under one strand for certain stitch effects.

CHAIN RING

Join a number of chain stitches into a ring with a slip stitch in the first chain. Work the first round of stitches around the chain and into the center. If the yarn end is also worked around, the ring is lightly padded and this end can be pulled to tighten it.

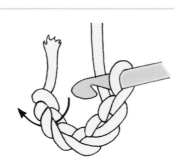

SLIP STITCH (SS)

Slip stitch has virtually no height and its main use is for joining, both for joining a chain ring, as shown, and for seaming (see page 33). It is also a means of carrying the yarn from one point to another without breaking the yarn.

Insert the hook from front to back under the top two strands of the required chain or stitch, yarn round hook, and pull it through both the work and the loop on the hook. One loop remains on the hook and one slip stitch has been made.

SINGLE CROCHET (SC)

Single crochet is a very useful short stitch, which is made in two steps.

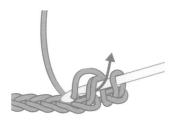 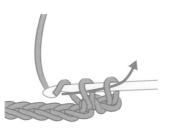

1 Insert the hook from front to back under the top two strands of the second chain from the hook or in the required stitch. Yarn round hook and pull it through, making two loops on the hook.

2 Yarn round hook and pull it through both loops, completing the single crochet and leaving one loop on the hook.

DOUBLE CROCHET (DC)

Double crochet is a taller stitch made with additional wraps.

 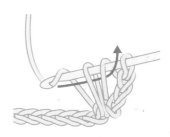

1 Yarn round hook before inserting the hook from front to back under the top two strands of the fourth chain from the hook or in the required stitch. Pull the yarn through to make three loops on the hook.

2 Yarn round hook and pull it through the first two loops on the hook.

3 Yarn round hook and pull it through the remaining two loops on the hook to complete the double crochet.

ADDITIONAL TECHNIQUES

It is sometimes easier to add small amounts of color afterward, rather than to include them in the knitting process.

DUPLICATE STITCH

This technique, sometimes called Swiss darning, is used to make color changes or additions to stockinette stitch. The new color covers the stitch exactly but adds to the thickness of the fabric, so it's better only used over small areas. Use a wool needle with a rounded point and work from right to left horizontally and from bottom to top vertically.

WORKING TO THE LEFT

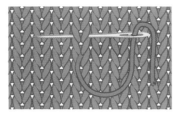

1 Thread the contrast color onto a wool needle, bring it out at the base of one v-shaped stitch, take it behind the two threads of the stitch above, and bring it out at the front.

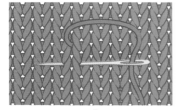

2 Tensioning the yarn carefully, insert the wool needle in the base of the stitch and bring it out at the base of the next stitch.

WORKING UPWARD

There are two different methods of covering stitches from row to row, but both give a similar result.

Using a wool needle, cover a stitch as in step 1 of working to the left, but bring the needle out in the stitch above. Over a large number of rows miss one stitch at regular intervals or the work will buckle.

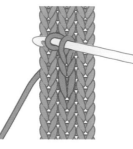

SURFACE CROCHET

Using a crochet hook and holding the yarn underneath the work, insert the hook in one stitch and pull a loop through. * Insert the hook in the next stitch above and pull a loop through both the work and the loop on the hook; repeat from *, missing one stitch at regular intervals.

Large French knots have been added to the Lily (page 80) and could be used in other floral designs.

FRENCH KNOTS

Making a nice round knot is a useful surface decoration that just needs a little practice.

1 Hold the yarn down with the left thumb and twist the wool needle twice around the taut yarn. For a larger knot, make an additional twist.

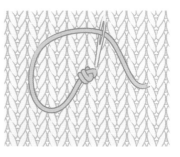

2 Still holding the yarn, pull the needle through the twists, insert it in the same place in the knitting, and pull it through to the wrong side.

PRESSING AND EDGING

Once you have completed your blocks, you will need to press them to shape and possibly add a border to frame the design.

PRESSING

It is important to pin out knitting and press it (called "blocking") to improve its regularity and stability. Pin it, right side down if it's untextured, preferably on a squared fabric over a soft surface such as a folded blanket. Use large quilting pins but beware of touching the plastic heads with a hot iron. Avoid raised areas and use steam if the yarn allows. Otherwise, simply damp and leave to dry.

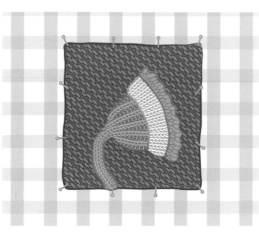

TIP

If you are pressing several blocks of the same size, use a waterproof marker pen to draw the outline on plain fabric and use this a template for pinning out each block.

ADDING A BORDER

A mitered garter stitch border frames a square block in a decorative way, and it is also useful for piecing by making the same number of stitches on all four sides.

A GARTER STITCH BORDER

Pick up and knit in each stitch of the cast-on edge, then work in garter stitch, increasing one stitch at each end of right-side rows and finally binding off knitwise on a wrong-side row. Noting that it will be necessary to skip some row-end stitches, pick up exactly the same number of stitches along the row ends as well as the bind-off edge and work them all in the same way. By maintaining this pattern of right-side row increases, a border can be made to almost any depth.

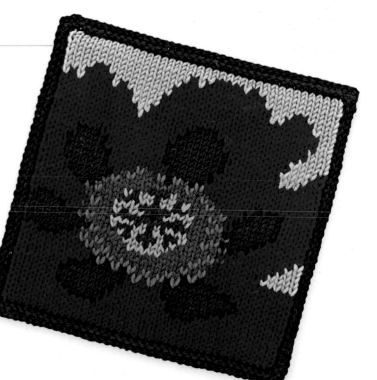

A narrow border was made around the Oriental Poppy (see page 108).

ASSEMBLING AND JOINING

Once you have completed your blocks, you will need to consider how to join them together.
As a general rule, use the darker yarn when seaming blocks of different colors or tones.

ASSEMBLING SQUARES

To assemble square blocks, join pairs until you have strips of the length or width measurement you require. Then join the strips into the finished square or rectangle.

PLAIN SQUARES

Infill squares can be made in stockinette stitch—fold the knitting diagonally from one corner to another to check that the sides match. Or they can be made in garter stitch, knitted from corner to corner by increasing one stitch at each end of right-side rows until the sides are the required measurement and then decreasing one stitch at each end of right-side rows.

The Cord Leaf block (page 65) was made using garter stitch knitted from corner to corner.

The Michaelmas Daisy block (page 79) was made using stockinette stitch.

SEWN SEAMS

OVER SEWING

Many of the square stockinette designs in this book have a textured edge made by casting on by the thumb method, binding off knitwise on the wrong side, and then picking up and binding off the same number of stitches along the row ends. In addition to texture, this produces the same number of stitches on all four edges.

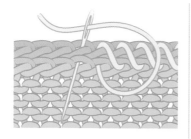

These are joined by over sewing on the wrong side, taking in single inside-edge strands only. The result is a very flat seam, as shown in the Pansy knitting bag (pages 120–121). It's not as strong as one taking in two strands along the edge.

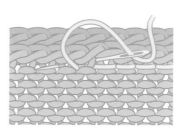

BACK STITCH

A very firm join can be made with back stitch on the wrong side, taking in two strands of each stitch. This may create a furrow on the right side, especially in stitches such as reverse stockinette stitch. Back stitch was used for the Leaf birdcage cover (pages 124–125) and then pressed thoroughly.

MATTRESS STITCH

If a textured edge is not required use invisible seaming, sometimes called mattress stitch, on the right side. With right sides facing and starting at the cast on, take the wool needle under the strand between the first and second stitches of one edge. Repeat at the other edge. Continue working into alternate edges, tightening the stitches as you go.

CROCHET SEAMS

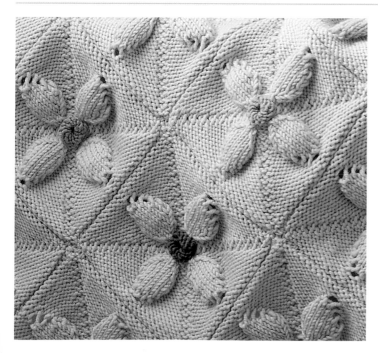

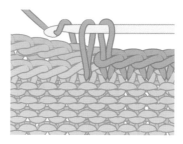

SINGLE CROCHET

Single crochet makes a very strong seam that is easier to work neatly on the wrong side as you have to miss occasional row ends to match the number of crochet stitches on all sides.

The furrow that this makes on the right side was used to enhance the quilted effect of the blocks in the Phlox baby blanket (pages 122–123).

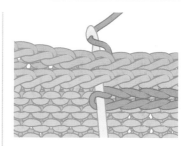

SLIP STITCH

A slightly less bulky seam, requiring less yarn, can be made using slip stitch instead of single crochet. This should always be worked on the wrong side as the ridge it makes is not very decorative.

2
INSTRUCTIONS

In this chapter you'll find written patterns as well as charts for intarsia and some lace designs. The blocks are organized into three sections: traditional, textured, and pictorial. The traditional section draws inspiration from old, lacy, floral knitting patterns, the textured section includes bobbles, loops, picots, and other textured stitches, and the pictorial section features some beautiful intarsia designs.

TRADITIONAL DESIGNS

In appearance, this flower has all the simplicity of a child's drawing, but it takes a little practice to keep the open stitches from closing up. Making each block in a different color would look very lively.

METHOD

Yarn DK cotton

Equipment 4 double-pointed knitting needles with an optional 5th needle

Cast on 2 sts on each of 3 needles. 6 sts.
1st round K.
Note Make the first yarn over on each needle in the usual way but work it very loosely.
2nd round [Yo, k1] 6 times. 12 sts.
3rd round [Yo, k2] 6 times. 18 sts.
4th round [Yo, k3] 6 times. 24 sts.
5th round [Yo, k4] 6 times. 30 sts.
6th round [Yo, k5] 6 times. 36 sts.
7th round [Yo, k6] 6 times. 42 sts.
8th round [Yo, k7] 6 times. 48 sts.
9th round [Yo, k8] 6 times. 54 sts.
10th round [Yo, k9] 6 times. 60 sts.
11th round [Yo, k10] 6 times. 66 sts.
12th round [Yo, k11] 6 times. 72 sts.
13th round [Yo, k12] 6 times. 78 sts.
14th round [Yo, k13] 6 times. 84 sts.
15th round [Yo, k14] 6 times. 90 sts.
** **16th round** K13, k2tog, turn.

Using 5th needle if preferred, continue in rows on these sts only.
1st row (WS) P14.
2nd row K12, k2tog. 13 sts.
3rd row P13.
4th row K11, k2tog. 12 sts.
5th row P12.
6th row K10, k2tog. 11 sts.
Bind off remaining sts purlwise.
RS facing, rejoin yarn and repeat from ** on each 15-st section.

2 LACE FLOWER
Advanced

Intense, old-fashioned patterning pulls the stitches this way and that to produce rounded petals, each outlined with smaller petals. Being hexagonal, this block is knitted using four double-pointed needles.

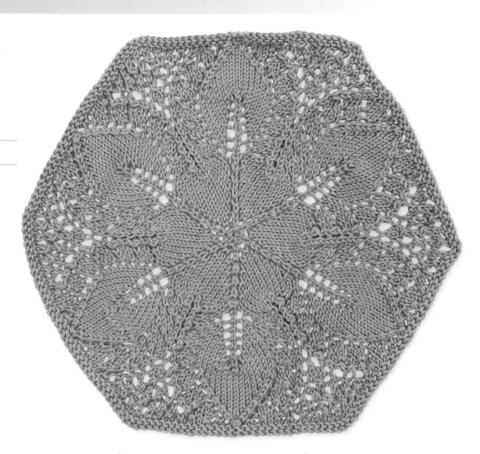

METHOD

Yarn Sport-weight cotton

Equipment 4 double-pointed knitting needles

Cast on 2 sts on each of 3 needles. 6 sts.
1st round K.
2nd round [Yo, k1] 6 times. 12 sts
3rd and alternate rounds K.
4th round [Yo, k1] 12 times. 24 sts.
6th round [Yo, k3, yo, k1] 6 times. 36 sts.
8th round [Yo, k5, yo, k1] 6 times. 48 sts.
10th round [Yo, k7, yo, k1] 6 times. 60 sts.
12th round [Yo, k9, yo, k1] 6 times. 72 sts.
14th round [Yo, k11, yo, k1] 6 times. 84 sts.
16th round * [Yo, k1] twice, yo, k2, k2tog, skpo, k1, k2tog, [yo, k1] 3 times; repeat from * 5 times. 102 sts.
18th round [Yo, k2, yo, k3, yo, k3tog, sk2po, yo, k3, yo, k2, yo, k1] 6 times. 114 sts.
20th round *Yo, k3, yo, k1, yo, [skpo, k1, k2tog] twice, yo, k1, yo, k3, yo, k1; repeat from * 5 times. 126 sts.
22nd round [Yo, k4, yo, k3, yo, k3tog, sk2po, yo, k3, yo, k4, yo, k1] 6 times. 138 sts.

24th round * Yo, k5, yo, k1, yo, [skpo, k1, k2tog] twice, yo, k1, yo, k5, yo, k1; repeat from * 5 times. 150 sts.
26th round [Yo, k6, yo, k3, yo, k3tog, sk2po, yo, k3, yo, k6, yo, k1] 6 times. 162 sts.
28th round * K5, k2tog, yo, k1, [yo, skpo, k1, k2tog] twice, yo, k1, yo, skpo, k6; repeat from * 5 times. 156 sts.
30th round [K4, k2tog, yo, k3, yo, k3tog, yo, k1, yo, sk2po, yo, k3, yo, skpo, k5] 6 times. 156 sts.
32nd round [K3, k2tog, yo, k1, yo, skpo, k1, k2tog, yo, k3, yo, skpo, k1,

k2tog, yo, k1, yo, skpo, k4] 6 times. 156 sts.
34th round * K2, k2tog, yo, k3, yo, k3tog, [yo, k1, yo, sk2po] twice, yo, k3, yo, skpo, k3; repeat from * 5 times. 156 sts.
36th round * K1, k2tog, yo, k1, yo, skpo, k1, [k2tog, yo, k1, yo] 3 times, skpo, k1, k2tog, yo, k1, yo, skpo, k2; repeat from * 5 times. 168 sts.
38th round [K2tog, yo, k3, yo, k3tog, yo, k1, yo, k2tog, yo, k1, yo, sk2po, yo, k1, yo, k2tog, yo, k1, yo, sk2po, yo, k3, yo, skpo, k1] 6 times. 180 sts.

39th round Slip first st, k to end of first needle then k first st from 2nd needle, k to end of 2nd needle then k first st from 3rd needle, k to end of 3rd needle then k slipped st from first needle.
40th round *Yo, k1, yo, skpo, k1, [k2tog, yo, k1, yo] twice, sk2po, yo, k1, yo, sk2po, k1, yo, k2tog, yo, k1, yo, skpo, k1, k2tog, yo, k1, yo, sk2po; repeat from * 5 times. 186 sts.
41st round P.
Turn and bind off loosely knitwise.

3 FLOWER BURST
Advanced

This design is for someone who has crochet as well as knitting skills, although the crochet required is very basic—it consists of two rounds to open up the center of the flower and then single crochet to make stitches to put on the needles. After that all the rounds are knitted.

METHOD

Yarn Sport-weight cotton

Equipment A crochet hook and 5 double-pointed knitting needles

Using crochet hook, make a slip ring (see page 25).
1st round 4ch, in ring [1dc, 1ch] 15 times, pull end to close ring, ss in 3rd ch of 4ch. 16 sts.
2nd round Ss in next ch sp, [6ch, miss 1ch sp, 1sc in next ch sp] 7 times, 6ch, miss 1ch sp, ss in same ch sp as first ss. 8 ch sp. One loop remains on hook. Loosen loop, pass ball of yarn through and pull tight. Now make sts to put on needles:
3rd round * In next ch sp [insert hook under ch, yrh, pull yarn through, yrh, pull yarn through loop on hook, slip loop just made from hook on to needle] 7 times, making 7 sts on needle. On the same needle make 7 sts in the next ch sp, totaling 14 sts on needle. ** Using the 2nd needle repeat from * to **, then repeat from * to ** using 3rd and 4th needles. 56 sts.

Continue in rounds using 5 double-pointed needles.
4th round [Yo, k7] 8 times. 64 sts.
5th and alternate rounds K.
6th round [Yo, k1, yo, k7] 8 times. 80 sts.
8th round [Yo, k3, yo, k7] 8 times. 96 sts.
10th round [Yo, k2tog, yo, k1, yo, skpo, yo, k7] 8 times. 112 sts.
12th round * Yo, k2tog, yo, k3, [yo, skpo] twice, k3, k2tog; repeat from * 7 times.
14th round * [Yo, k2tog] twice, yo, k1, [yo, skpo] 3 times, k1, k2tog; repeat from * 7 times.
16th round * [Yo, k2tog] twice, yo, k3, [yo, skpo] twice, yo, s2kpo; repeat from * 7 times.
18th round P.
Turn and bind off loosely knitwise.

4 OPEN BLOOM
Intermediate

A ring of bobbles creates the center of this flower and then simple increases cause the pointed petals to spiral outward. The resulting block can be treated as a circle or an octagon, depending on how it is pressed and used.

METHOD

Yarn Sport-weight cotton

Equipment 5 double-pointed knitting needles

Specific abbreviation
mb make bobble: (k1, p1, k1) in next st, turn, p3, turn, pass 2nd and 3rd sts over first st, k this st tbl.

Cast on 2 sts on each of 4 needles.
8 sts.
K 2 rounds.
3rd round [Yo, k1] 8 times. 16 sts.
4th and alternate rounds K.
5th round [Yo, k2] 8 times. 24 sts.
7th round [Yo, k1, mb, k1] 8 times.
32 sts.
9th round [Yo, k4] 8 times. 40 sts.
11th round [Yo, k5] 8 times. 48 sts.
13th round [Yo, k6] 8 times. 56 sts.
15th round [Yo, k7] 8 times. 64 sts.
17th round [Yo, k8] 8 times. 72 sts.
(18 sts on each needle).

19th round [Yo, k1, yo, k2tog, k6]
8 times. 80 sts.
21st round [Yo, k3, yo, k2tog, k5]
8 times. 88 sts.
23rd round [Yo, k5, yo, k2tog, k4]
8 times. 96 sts.
25th round [Yo, k7, yo, k2tog, k3]
8 times. 104 sts.
27th round [Yo, k9, yo, k2tog, k2]
8 times. 112 sts.
29th round [Yo, k11, yo, k2tog, k1]
8 times. 120 sts.
31st round [Yo, k13, yo, k2tog]
8 times. 128 sts.
(32 sts on each needle).
33rd round P.
Turn and bind off loosely knitwise.

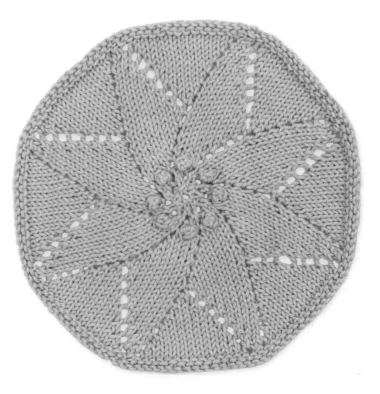

5 SISYRINCHIUM
Intermediate

Starting at the outer edge and working toward the middle makes this block different from most hexagons. The result is a chunky and well-defined flower with a neat center.

METHOD

Yarn Sport-weight cotton

Equipment 4 double-pointed knitting needles

Cast on 44 sts on each of 3 needles. 132 sts.
1st round K.
2nd round [K1, p2tog, p16, p2tog, k1] 6 times. 120 sts.
3rd round [K1, p18, k1] 6 times.
4th round [K1, k2tog, k14, skpo, k1] 6 times. 108 sts.
5th and 6th rounds K.
7th round [K1, p2tog, p12, p2tog, k1] 6 times. 96 sts.
8th round [K1, p7, yo, p7, k1] 6 times. 102 sts.
9th round [K1, p7, k1, p7, k1] 6 times.
10th round [K1, p2tog, p5, yo, k1, yo, p5, p2tog, k1] 6 times.
11th round [K1, p6, k3, p6, k1] 6 times.
12th round [K1, p6, yo, k3, yo, p6, k1] 6 times. 114 sts.
13th round [K1, p2tog, p4, k5, p4, p2tog, k1] 6 times. 102 sts.
14th round [K1, p5, yo, k5, yo, p5, k1] 6 times. 114 sts.
15th round [K1, p5, k7, p5, k1] 6 times.
16th round [K1, p2tog, p3, yo, k7, yo, p3, p2tog, k1] 6 times.
17th round [K1, p4, k9, p4, k1] 6 times.

18th round [K1, p4, k3, s2kpo, k3, p4, k1] 6 times. 102 sts.
19th round [K1, p2tog, p2, k7, p2, p2tog, k1] 6 times. 90 sts.
20th round [K1, p3, k2, sk2po, k2, p3, k1] 6 times. 78 sts.
21st round [K1, p3, k5, p3, k1] 6 times.
22nd round [K1, p2tog, p1, k1, sk2po, k1, p1, p2tog, k1] 6 times. 54 sts.
23rd round [K1, p2, k3, p2, k1] 6 times.
24th round [K1, p2, sk2po, p2, k1] 6 times. 42 sts.
25th round [K1, p2tog, k1, p2tog, k1] 6 times. 30 sts.
26th round [K1, s2kpo, k1] 6 times. 18 sts.
27th round [S2kpo] 6 times. 6 sts. Break the yarn, draw it through the remaining 6 sts and pull tight.

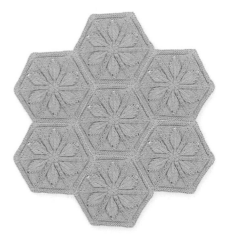

Tessellation

6 LEAF DIAMOND
Advanced

Four small leaves sit tightly in the center of a reverse stockinette stitch square that is knitted from corner to corner. This means the instructions look lengthy but it makes a very neat little block.

METHOD

Yarn Sport-weight wool

Equipment A pair of knitting needles

Cast on 3 sts.
1st row (RS) P.
2nd row [Kfb] twice, k1. 5 sts.
3rd row P.
4th row Kfb, k2, kfb, k1. 7 sts.
5th row P.
6th row Kfb, k4, kfb, k1. 9 sts.
7th row P.
8th row Kfb, k6, kfb, k1. 11 sts.
9th row P5, (k1, p1, k1) in next st, p5. 13 sts.
10th row Kfb, k4, p3, k3, kfb, k1. 15 sts.
11th row P6, k1, [yo, k1] twice, p6. 17 sts.
12th row Kfb, k5, p5, k4, kfb, k1. 19 sts.
13th row P7, k2, yo, k1, yo, k2, p7. 21 sts.
14th row Kfb, k6, p7, k5, kfb, k1. 23 sts.
15th row P5, (k1, p1, k1) in next st, p2, skpo, k3, k2tog, p2, (k1, p1, k1) in next st, p5. 25 sts.
16th row Kfb, k4, p3, k2, p5, k2, p3, k3, kfb, k1. 27 sts.
17th row P6, k1, [yo, k1] twice, p2, skpo, k1, k2tog, p2, k1, [yo, k1] twice, p6. 29 sts.
18th row Kfb, k5, p5, k2, p3, k2, p5, k4, kfb, k1. 31 sts.
19th row P7, k2, yo, k1, yo, k2, p2, sk2po, p2, k2, yo, k1, yo, k2, p7. 33 sts.
20th row Kfb, k6, [p7, k5] twice, kfb, k1. 35 sts.
21st row P8, skpo, k3, k2tog, p2, (k1, p1, k1) in next st, p2, skpo, k3, k2tog, p8. 33 sts.
22nd row K1, k2tog, k5, p5, k2, p3, k2, p5, k5, k2tog, k1. 31 sts.
23rd row P7, skpo, k1, k2tog, p2, k1, [yo, k1] twice, p2, skpo, k1, k2tog, p7. 29 sts.
24th row K1, k2tog, k4, p3, k2, p5, k2, p3, k4, k2tog, k1. 27 sts.
25th row P6, sk2po, p2, k2, yo, k1, yo, k2, p2, sk2po, p6. 25 sts.
26th row K1, k2tog, k6, p7, k6, k2tog, k1. 23 sts.
27th row P8, skpo, k3, k2tog, p8. 21 sts.
28th row K1, k2tog, k5, p5, k5, k2tog, k1. 19 sts.
29th row P7, skpo, k1, k2tog, p7. 17 sts.
30th row K1, k2tog, k4, p3, k4, k2tog, k1. 15 sts.
31st row P6, sk2po, p6. 13 sts.
32nd row K1, k2tog, k7, k2tog, k1. 11 sts.
33rd row P.
34th row K1, k2tog, k5, k2tog, k1. 9 sts.
35th row P.
36th row K1, k2tog, k3, k2tog, k1. 7 sts.
37th row P1, [p2tog, p1] twice. 5 sts.
38th row K1, sk2po, k1. 3 sts.
39th row P3tog.
Fasten off remaining one st.

7 **FOUR SEASONS**
Advanced

Four very full, heavily embossed leaves crowd the corner of this triangle, so that a joined square contains a cluster of sixteen leaves. This could be set among plain squares for emphasis.

METHOD

Yarn Sport-weight cotton in 3 shades of one color

Equipment A pair of knitting needles

Specific abbreviation
kpk (k1, p1, k1) in next st to make 3 sts from one.

Make 4 triangles.
Cast on 2 sts.
1st row (RS) Kfb, k1. 3 sts.
2nd row [Kfb] twice, k1. 5 sts.
3rd row K2, kpk, k2. 7 sts.
4th row K2, p3, k2.
5th row Kfb, k2, [yo, k1] twice, kfb, k1. 11 sts.
6th row K3, p5, k3.
7th row Kfb, k4, yo, k1, yo, k3, kfb, k1. 15 sts.
8th row K4, p7, k4.
9th row Kfb, k6, yo, k1, yo, k5, kfb, k1. 19 sts.

10th row K5, p9, k5.
11th row Kfb, k8, yo, k1, yo, k7, kfb, k1. 23 sts.
12th row K6, p11, k6.
13th row Kfb, k10, yo, k1, yo, k9, kfb, k1. 27 sts.
14th row K7, p13, k7.
15th row Kfb, k12, yo, k1, yo, k11, kfb, k1. 31 sts.
16th row K8, p15, k8.
17th row Kfb, k2, kpk, k4, skpo, k11, k2tog, k4, kpk, k1, kfb, k1. 35 sts.
18th row K4, p3, k4, p13, k4, p3, k4.
19th row Kfb, k4, yo, k1, yo, k5, skpo, k9, k2tog, k5, yo, k1, yo, k3, kfb, k1. 39 sts.
20th row K5, p5, k4, p11, k4, p5, k5.
21st row Kfb, k6, yo, k1, yo, k6, skpo, k7, k2tog, k6, yo, k1, yo, k5, kfb, k1. 43 sts.
22nd row K6, p7, k4, p9, k4, p7, k6.
23rd row Kfb, k8, yo, k1, yo, k7, skpo, k5, k2tog, k7, yo, k1, yo, k7, kfb, k1. 47 sts.

24th row K7, p9, k4, p7, k4, p9, k7.
25th row Kfb, k10, yo, k1, yo, k8, skpo, k3, k2tog, k8, yo, k1, yo, k9, kfb, k1. 51 sts.
26th row K8, p11, k4, p5, k4, p11, k8.
27th row Kfb, k12, yo, k1, yo, k9, skpo, k1, k2tog, k9, yo, k1, yo, k11, kfb, k1. 55 sts.
28th row K9, p13, k4, p3, k4, p13, k9.
29th row Kfb, k14, yo, k1, yo, k10, s2kpo, k10, yo, k1, yo, k13, kfb, k1. 59 sts.
30th row K10, p15, k4, p1, k4, p15, k10.
31st row Kfb, k9, skpo, k11, k2tog, k4, kpk, k4, skpo, k11, k2tog, k8, kfb, k1.
32nd row K11, p13, k4, p3, k4, p13, k11.
33rd row Kfb, k10, skpo, k9, k2tog, k5, yo, k1, yo, k5, skpo, k9, k2tog, k9, kfb, k1.

34th row K12, p11, k4, p5, k4, p11, k12.
35th row Kfb, k11, skpo, k7, k2tog, k6, yo, k1, yo, k6, skpo, k7, k2tog, k10, kfb, k1.
36th row K13, p9, k4, p7, k4, p9, k13.
37th row Kfb, k12, skpo, k5, k2tog, k7, yo, k1, yo, k7, skpo, k5, k2tog, k11, kfb, k1.
38th row K14, p7, k4, p9, k4, p7, k14.
39th row Kfb, k13, skpo, k3, k2tog, k8, yo, k1, yo, k8, skpo, k3, k2tog, k12, kfb, k1.
40th row K15, p5, k4, p11, k4, p5, k15.
41st row Kfb, k14, skpo, k1, k2tog, k9, yo, k1, yo, k9, skpo, k1, k2tog, k13, kfb, k1.
42nd row K16, p3, k4, p13, k4, p3, k16.
43rd row Kfb, k15, s2kpo, k10, yo, k1, yo, k10, s2kpo, k14, kfb, k1.

44th row K22, p15, k22.
45th row Kfb, k21, skpo, k11, k2tog, k20, kfb, k1.
46th row K23, p13, k23.
47th row Kfb, k22, skpo, k9, k2tog, k21, kfb, k1.
48th row K24, p11, k24.
49th row Kfb, k23, skpo, k7, k2tog, k22, kfb, k1.
50th row K25, p9, k25.
51st row Kfb, k24, skpo, k5, k2tog, k23, kfb, k1.
52nd row K26, p7, k26.
53rd row Kfb, k25, skpo, k3, k2tog, k24, kfb, k1.
54th row K27, p5, k27.
55th row Kfb, k26, skpo, k1, k2tog, k25, kfb, k1.
56th row K28, p3, k28.
57th row Kfb, k27, s2kpo, k26, kfb, k1.
58th row K.
59th row Kfb, k56, kfb, k1. 61 sts. Bind off knitwise.

Making up Taking in half a stitch from each edge, join triangles to form a square.

8 QUARTO LEAF
Beginner

This quarter of a square block contains a single well-defined leaf. Assemble four triangles to turn the leaves into petals. A mixture of garter stitch, stockinette stitch, reverse stockinette stitch, and eyelets add up to a richly textured piece.

METHOD

Yarn DK cotton in 4 shades of one color

Equipment A pair of knitting needles

Make 4 triangles, one in each shade. Cast on 3 sts.
1st row (RS) [Kfb] twice, k1. 5 sts.
2nd row P.
3rd row Kfb, p1, yo, k1, yo, pfb, k1. 9 sts.
4th row P1, k1, p5, k1, p1.
5th row Kfb, p3, yo, k1, yo, p2, pfb, k1. 13 sts.
6th row P1, k2, p7, k2, p1.
7th row Kfb, p5, yo, k1, yo, p4, pfb, k1. 17 sts.
8th row P1, k3, p9, k3, p1.
9th row Kfb, p7, yo, k1, yo, p6, pfb, k1. 21 sts.
10th row P1, k4, p11, k4, p1.
11th row Kfb, p9, yo, k1, yo, p8, pfb, k1. 25 sts.
12th row P1, k5, p13, k5, p1.
13th row Kfb, p11, yo, k1, yo, p10, pfb, k1. 29 sts.
14th row P1, k6, p15, k6, p1.
15th row Kfb, p6, skpo, k11, k2tog, p5, pfb, k1.
16th row P1, k7, p13, k7, p1.
17th row Kfb, p7, skpo, k9, k2tog, p6, pfb, k1.

18th row P1, k8, p11, k8, p1.
19th row Kfb, p8, skpo, k7, k2tog, p7, pfb, k1.
20th row P1, k9, p9, k9, p1.
21st row Kfb, p9, skpo, k5, k2tog, p8, pfb, k1.
22nd row P1, k10, p7, k10, p1.
23rd row Kfb, p10, skpo, k3, k2tog, p9, pfb, k1.
24th row P1, k11, p5, k11, p1.
25th row Kfb, p11, skpo, k1, k2tog, p10, pfb, k1.
26th row P1, k12, p3, k12, p1.
27th row Kfb, p12, s2kpo, p11, pfb, k1.
28th row P1, k27, p1.
29th row K1, [yo twice, s2kpo] 9 times, yo twice, k1. 31 sts.
30th row P1, (k1, p1) in double yo, [k1, (k1, p1) in double yo] 9 times, p1.
31st row K1, p29, k1.
Bind off knitwise.

Making up Right sides facing and taking in half a stitch from each edge, join triangles with mattress stitch (see page 33).

9 SPRING GREENS
Intermediate

Adding bobbles to stockinette stitch and lace makes a lively kaleidoscope when these four triangles are joined. It's a design that isn't too difficult to follow because of the logical progression of the stitches.

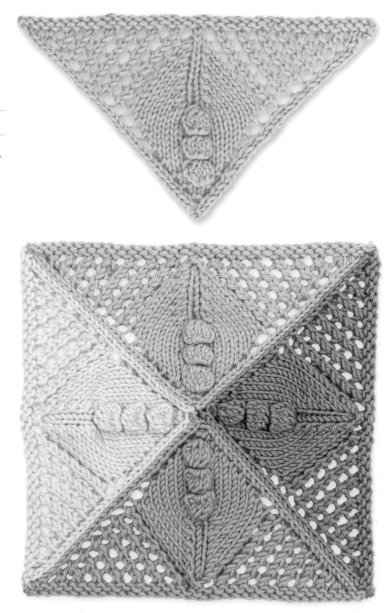

METHOD

Yarn DK wool in 4 shades of one color

Equipment A pair of knitting needles

Specific abbreviations
mb make bobble: (k1, p1, k1, p1, k1) in next st, turn, p5, turn, k5, turn, p5, turn, pass 2nd, 3rd, 4th and 5th sts over first st, k this st through back of loop;

Make 4 triangles, one in each shade. Cast on 2 sts.
1st row (RS) Kfb, k1. 3 sts.
2nd row Pfb, p2. 4 sts.
3rd row K2, yo, k2. 5 sts.
4th and WS rows P.
5th row K2, yo, k1, yo, k2. 7 sts.
7th row K2, yo, k3, yo, k2. 9 sts.
9th row K2, yo, k5, yo, k2. 11 sts.
11th row K2, yo, k3, mb, k3, yo, k2. 13 sts.
13th row K2, yo, k9, yo, k2. 15 sts.
15th row K2, yo, k5, mb, k5, yo, k2. 17 sts.
17th row K2, yo, k13, yo, k2. 19 sts.
19th row K2, yo, k7, mb, k7, yo, k2. 21 sts.
21st row K2, yo, k1, yo, k5, ssk, k1, k2tog, k5, yo, k1, yo, k2. 23 sts.
23rd row K2, yo, k1, yo, ssk, yo, k4, ssk, k1, k2tog, k4, yo, k2tog, yo, k1, yo, k2. 25 sts.

25th row K2, yo, k1, [yo, ssk] twice, yo, k3, ssk, k1, k2tog, k3, [yo, k2tog] twice, yo, k1, yo, k2. 27 sts.
27th row K2, yo, k1, [yo, ssk] 3 times, yo, k2, ssk, k1, k2tog, k2, [yo, k2tog] 3 times, yo, k1, yo, k2. 29 sts.
29th row K2, yo, k1, [yo, ssk] 4 times, yo, k1, ssk, k1, k2tog, k1, [yo, k2tog] 4 times, yo, k1, yo, k2. 31 sts.
31st row K2, yo, k1, [yo, ssk] 6 times, k1, k2tog, [yo, k2tog] 5 times, yo, k1, yo, k2. 33 sts.
33rd row K2, yo, k1, [yo, ssk] 6 times, yo, sk2po, [yo, k2tog] 6 times, yo, k1, yo, k2. 35 sts.
35th row P.
Bind off knitwise.

Making up Taking in one stitch from each edge and with bobbles to center, join triangles to form a square.

10 HYDRANGEA
Beginner

A cluster of four large bobbles on each section of this square join up to make a flower-like center. It is reminiscent of the larger and more elaborate quilt squares of the nineteenth century.

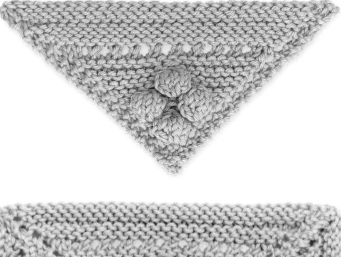

METHOD

Yarn Sport weight cotton

Equipment A pair of knitting needles

Specific abbreviation
mb make bobble: (k1, yo, k1, yo, k1) in next st to make 5 sts from one, turn, [p5, turn, k5, turn] twice, p1, [p2tog] twice, turn, sk2po.

Note Slip stitches are slipped knitwise.

Make 4 sections.
Cast on 2 sts.
1st row (RS) Kfb, k1. 3 sts.
2nd row Slip 1, kfb, k1. 4 sts.
3rd row Slip 1, k3.
4th row Slip 1, k1, yo, k2. 5 sts.
5th row Slip 1, k4.
6th row Slip 1, [k1, yo] twice, k2, 7 sts.
7th row Slip 1, k6.
8th row Slip 1, k1, yo, k3, yo, k2. 9 sts.
9th row Slip 1, k8.
10th row Slip 1, k1, yo, k5, yo, k2. 11 sts.
11th row Slip 1, k10.
12th row Slip 1, k1, yo, k7, yo, k2. 13 sts.
13th row Slip 1, k5, mb, k6.
14th row Slip 1, k1, yo, k9, yo, k2. 15 sts.
15th row Slip 1, k14.

16th row Slip 1, k1, yo, k11, yo, k2. 17 sts.
17th row Slip 1, k5, mb, k3, mb, k6.
18th row Slip 1, k1, yo, k13, yo, k2. 19 sts.
19th row Slip 1, k18.
20th row Slip 1, k1, yo, k15, yo, k2. 21 sts.
21st row Slip 1, k9, mb, k10.
22nd row Slip 1, k1, yo, k17, yo, k2. 23 sts.
23rd row Slip 1, k22.
24th row Slip 1, k1, yo, k19, yo, k2. 25 sts.
25th row Slip 1, k24.
26th row Slip 1, k1, yo, p2, [yo, p2tog] 9 times, p1, yo, k2. 27 sts.
27th row Slip 1, k26.
28th row Slip 1, k1, yo, k23, yo, k2. 29 sts.
29th row Slip 1, k1, p25, k2.
30th row Slip 1, k1, yo, p25, yo, k2. 31 sts.
31st row Slip 1, k30.
32nd row Slip 1, k1, yo, k27, yo, k2. 33 sts.
33rd row Slip 1, k1, p29, k2.
Bind off knitwise.

Making up With cast-on to center and taking in one stitch from each section, join sections to form a square.

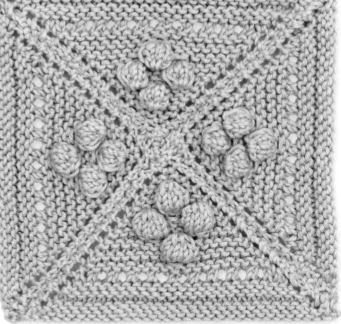

11 LEAF QUARTET
Advanced

The corner-to-corner construction of these segments makes an unusual diagonal design. Each piece looks rather elliptical but squares up when four are joined together. You could, of course, use a single color.

METHOD

Yarn DK wool in green (A) and turquoise (B)

Equipment A pair of knitting needles

Make 4 segments.
Using A, cast on 3 sts.
1st row (RS) K.
2nd row K1, p1, k1.
3rd row [Kfb] twice, k1. 5 sts.
Note Taking yarn to the opposite side of the work as necessary, use stranding technique for 4th–6th rows, then use intarsia technique (see page 26).
4th row KfbA, k1A, p1B, kfbA, k1A. 7 sts.
5th row KfbA, p1A, k3B, pfbA, k1A. 9 sts.
6th row K3A, p3B, k3A.
7th row K2A, p1A, using B: [k1, yo] twice, k1; p1A, k2A. 11 sts.
8th row K3A, p5B, k3A.
9th row K2A, p1A, using B: k2, yo, k1, yo, k2; p1A, k2A. 13 sts.
10th row K2A, kfbA, p7B, kfbA, k2A. 15 sts.
11th row K2A, p2A, using B: k3, yo, k1, yo, k3; p2A, k2A. 17 sts.
12th row K4A, p9B, k4A.
13th row K2A, p2A, using B: k4, yo, k1, yo, k4; p2A, k2A. 19 sts.
14th row K3A, kfbA, p11B, kfbA, k3A. 21 sts.
15th row K2A, p3A, using B: k5, yo, k1, yo, k5; p3A, k2A. 23 sts.

16th row K5A, p13B, k5A.
17th row K2A, p3A, using B: k6, yo, k1, yo, k6; p3A, k2A. 25 sts.
18th row K4A, kfbA, p15B, kfbA, k4A. 27 sts.
19th row K1A, kfbA, p4A, using B: k7, yo, k1, yo, k7; p4A, pfbA, k1A. 29 sts.
20th row K7A, p17B, k7A.
21st row K1A, k2togA, p4A, using B: k7, s2kpo, k7; p4A, k2togA, k1A. 27 sts.
22nd row K4A, k2togA, p15B, k2togA, k4A. 25 sts.
23rd row K2A, p3A, using B: k6, s2kpo, k6; p3A, k2A. 23 sts.
24th row As 16th row.
25th row K2A, p3A, using B: k5, s2kpo, k5; p3A, k2A. 21 sts.
26th row K3A, k2togA, p11B, k2togA, k3A. 19 sts.
27th row K2A, p2A, using B: k4, s2kpo, k4; p2A, k2A. 17 sts.
28th row As 12th row.
29th row K2A, p2A, using B: k3, s2kpo, k3; p2A, k2A. 15 sts.
30th row K2A, k2togA, p7B, k2togA, k2A. 13 sts.
31st row K2A, p1A, using B: k2, s2kpo, k2; p1A, k2A. 11 sts.
32nd row As 8th row.
33rd row K2A, p1A, using B: k1, s2kpo, k1; p1A, k2A. 9 sts.
34th row As 6th row.
Continue with A.
35th row K2, p1, s2kpo, p1, k2. 7 sts.

36th row K1, k2tog, p1, k2tog, k1. 5 sts.
37th row K2tog, p1, k2tog. 3 sts.
38th row Sk2po.
Fasten off. Square up and press edges only.

Making up With cast-on to center, taking in half a stitch from each edge, join segments to form a square.

12 THICKET
Advanced

Densely patterned with small embossed leaves, this square is knitted in the round using five double-pointed needles—although the corners are at the center of the needles and not at the ends.

METHOD

Yarn DK wool

Equipment 5 double-pointed knitting needles

Cast on one st on each of 4 needles. 4 sts.
1st round K.
2nd round [Yo, k1] 4 times. 8 sts.
3rd round K.
4th round [Yo, k1, yo, p1] 4 times. 16 sts.
5th round [P1, k1, p2] 4 times.
6th round [P1, yo, k1, yo, p2] 4 times. 24 sts.
7th round [P2, k1, p3] 4 times.
8th round [P2, yo, k1, yo] 8 times. 40 sts.
9th round [P3, k1, p3, k3] 4 times.
10th round * P3, yo, k1, yo, p3, [k1, yo] twice, k1; repeat from * 3 times. 56 sts.
11th round [P4, k1, p4, k5] 4 times.
12th round [P4, yo, k1, yo, p4, k2, yo, k1, yo, k2] 4 times. 72 sts.
13th round [P5, k1, p5, k7] 4 times.
14th round * [P2, yo, k1, yo] 3 times, p2, ssk, s2kpo, k2tog; repeat from * 3 times. 80 sts.
15th round [P2, k3, p3, k1, p3, k3,

p2, s2kpo] 4 times. 72 sts.
16th round * P2, [k1, yo] twice, k1, p3, yo, k1, yo, p3, [k1, yo] twice, k1, p3; repeat from * 3 times. 96 sts.
17th round [P2, k5, p4, k1, p4, k5, p3] 4 times.
18th round [P2, k2, yo, k1, yo, k2, p4, yo, k1, yo, p4, k2, yo, k1, yo, k2, p3] 4 times. 120 sts.
19th round [P2, k7, p5, k1, p5, k7, p3] 4 times.
20th round * P2, ssk, s2kpo, k2tog, p2, [yo, k1, yo, p2] 3 times, ssk, s2kpo, k2tog, p2, yo, k1, yo; repeat from * 3 times.
21st round [P2, s2kpo, p2, k3, p3, k1, p3, k3, p2, s2kpo, p2, k3] 4 times. 104 sts.
22nd round * P5, [k1, yo] twice, k1, p3, yo, k1, yo, p3, [k1, yo] twice, k1, p5, [k1, yo] twice, k1; repeat from * 3 times. 136 sts.
23rd round [P5, k5, p4, k1, p4, k5, p5, k5] 4 times.
24th round [P5, k2, yo, k1, yo, k2, p4, yo, k1, yo, p4, k2, yo, k1, yo, k2, p5, k2, yo, k1, yo, k2] 4 times. 168 sts.
25th round * P5, k7, p5, k1, [p5, k7] twice; repeat from * 3 times.

26th round * P5, ssk, s2kpo, k2tog, p5, yo, k1, yo, [p5, ssk, s2kpo, k2tog] twice; repeat from * 3 times. 128 sts.
27th round [P5, s2kpo, p6, k1, p6, s2kpo, p5, s2kpo] 4 times. 104 sts.
28th round [P12, yo, k1, yo, p13] 4 times. 112 sts.
29th round K.
Bind off knitwise.

13 PHLOX
Intermediate

Simplicity is the key feature of this flower with four plump petals. It's knitted in the round from the outside edges to the center, finishing with an effect like a small button.

METHOD

Yarn DK wool

Equipment 5 double-pointed knitting needles

Cast on 23 sts on each of 4 needles. 92 sts.
1st round P.
2nd round [P2tog, p19, p2tog] 4 times. 84 sts.
3rd round P.
4th round [P2tog, p8, yo, p2tog, p7, p2tog] 4 times. 76 sts.
5th round [P9, k1, p9] 4 times.
6th round [P2tog, p7, yo, k1, yo, p7, p2tog] 4 times.
7th round [P8, k3, p8] 4 times.
8th round [P2tog, p6, yo, k3, yo, p6, p2tog] 4 times.
9th round [P7, k5, p7] 4 times.
10th round [P2tog, p5, yo, k5, yo, p5, p2tog] 4 times.
11th round [P6, k7, p6] 4 times.
12th round [P2tog, p4, yo, k7, yo, p4, p2tog] 4 times.

13th round [P5, k9, p5] 4 times.
14th round [P2tog, p3, ssk, k5, k2tog, p3, p2tog] 4 times. 60 sts.
15th round [P4, k7, p4] 4 times.
16th round [P2tog, p2, ssk, k3, k2tog, p2, p2tog] 4 times. 44 sts.
17th round [P3, k5, p3] 4 times.
18th round [P2tog, p1, ssk, k1, k2tog, p1, p2tog] 4 times. 28 sts.
19th round [P2, k3, p2] 4 times.
20th round [P2tog, s2kpo, p2tog] 4 times. 12 sts. ******
21st, 22nd, and 23rd rounds P.
Break yarn, thread end on to a wool needle, draw through remaining stitches, pull tight, and fasten off.

Variation
This block can be given a contrast center, as shown in the baby blanket on pages 122–123. Work as above to ******, then continue, using a contrast color:
21st round K.
22nd, 23rd, and 24th rounds P.
Break yarn, thread end on to wool needle, draw through remaining stitches, pull tight, and fasten off.

14 LACE BOUQUET
Intermediate

Three small bobbles enhance the openwork of this motif. The curving stems are created by changing from patterning on right-side rows to patterning on both sides of the work. It is a companion to Buttonhole (page 51).

Stitch Key

☐ k on RS, p on WS

● k on WS

○ yarn over needle

◿ k2tog on RS, p2tog on WS

◺ skpo on RS, p2tog tbl on WS

◭ s2kpo

B make bobble: (k1, yo, k1) in one st, turn, p3, turn, pass 2nd and 3rd sts over first st, k this st tbl

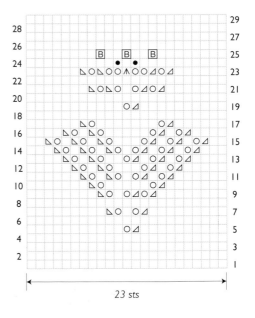

METHOD

Yarn Sport-weight cotton

Equipment A pair of knitting needles

Cast on 23 sts by the thumb method (see page 24). Beginning with a k row, work in st-st from the chart, reading RS rows from right to left and WS rows from left to right, as indicated by row numbering. When 29th row has been completed, bind off knitwise.

To neaten the sides, RS facing, pick up and k23 sts along one edge then bind off knitwise. Do the same along the second edge.

23 sts

15 BUTTONHOLE
Intermediate

A companion to Lace Bouquet (page 50), this lacy little flower has patterning on both right-side and wrong-side rows to give fluidity to a perfectly symmetrical design.

Stitch Key

☐ k on RS, p on WS

● k on WS

O yarn over needle

↗ k2sso

◣ sk2po

◿ k2tog on RS, p2tog on WS

◺ skpo on RS, p2tog tbl on WS

◥ k1 tbl

⋀ s2kpo

METHOD

Yarn Sport-weight cotton

Equipment A pair of knitting needles

Cast on 23 sts by the thumb method (see page 24).
Beginning with a k row, work in st-st from the chart, reading RS rows from right to left and WS rows from left to right, as indicated by row numbering.
When 29th row has been completed, bind off knitwise.

To neaten the sides, RS facing, pick up and k23 sts along one edge then bind off knitwise. Do the same along the second edge.

Mix and Match 14 + 15

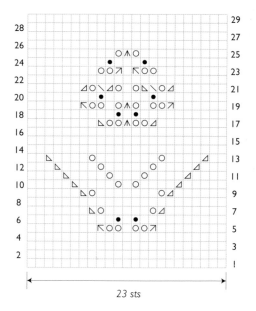

23 sts

TEXTURED DESIGNS

The leaves of this little motif require a slightly different long-stitch technique to that used for the petals of the bachelor's button (page 53), while the bud is a sort of elaborate bobble.

METHOD

Yarn Worsted-weight wool in soft white (A), blue-green (B), and mauve (C)

Equipment A pair of knitting needles

Using A, cast on 15 sts by the thumb method (see page 24).
1st and 3rd rows K.
2nd and 4th rows P.
Note Strand color not in use (see page 26)
5th row K7A, k1B, k7A.
6th row P7A, p1B, p7A.
Repeat 5th and 6th rows once more.
9th row K3A, insert right-hand needle in space to right of first center st B (on 5th row), pull through a loop of B, using A: k next st then pass loop over this st without twisting it, k3A, k1B, k3A, insert right-hand needle in space to left of first center st B, pull through a loop of B, using A: k next st then pass loop over this st without twisting it, k3A.

10th row P7A, p1B, p7A.
11th row K7A, using B: [k1, yo, k1, yo, k1, yo, k1] in next st, k7A. 21 sts.
12th row P7A, p7C, p7A.
13th row K7A, using C: ssk, s2kpo, k2tog, k7A. 17 sts.
14th row P7A, p3togC, p7A. 15 sts. Continue with A.
15th and 17th rows K.
16th and 18th rows P.
19th row K.
Bind off knitwise.

To neaten the sides, RS facing and using A, pick up and k15 sts along one edge then bind off knitwise. Do the same along the second edge.

17 BACHELOR'S BUTTON
Intermediate

The petals of this bachelor's button are long dropped stitches picked up on subsequent rows. It can be used as part of an all-over pattern, but here it's used as a single motif.

METHOD

Yarn Worsted-weight wool in yellow (A) and blue (B)

Equipment A pair of knitting needles

Using A, cast on 15 sts by the thumb method (see page 24).
1st and 3rd rows (RS) K.
2nd and 4th rows P.
Note Strand color not in use (see page 26).
5th and 7th rows K7A, k1B, k7A.
6th and 8th rows P7A, p1B, p7A.
9th row K7A, using B: [k1, yo, k1, yo, k1] in next st, k7A. 19 sts.
10th row P7A, using B: p5 wrapping yarn twice for each st, p7A.
11th row K3A, wyab slip next 4 sts A, drop first long st B to front, slip same 4 sts A back on to left-hand needle, pick up dropped st B and slip it back on to left-hand needle without twisting it, using A:

k2tog tbl (ie the long st and the next st), k3A, dropping extra wraps, wyab slip next 3 sts B, drop last st B to front, wyab slip 4 sts A, slip dropped st B on to left-hand needle without twisting it, slip 4 sts A back on to left-hand needle, k3A, k2togA (ie the next st and the long st), k3A. 17 sts.
12th row P7A, wyif slip next 3 sts B, p7A.
13th row K4A, wyab slip next 3 sts A, drop first long st B to front, slip same 3 sts A back on to left-hand needle, pick up dropped st B and slip it back on to left-hand needle without twisting it, k2tog tbl A, k2A, wyab slip the next st B, drop next st B to front, slip 3 sts A, slip st B on to left-hand needle without twisting it, slip same 3 sts A back on to left-hand needle, k2A, k2togA, k4A. 15 sts.
Continue with A.

14th, 16th, and 18th rows P.
15th, 17th, and 19th rows K.
Bind off knitwise.

To neaten the sides, RS facing and using A, pick up and k15 sts along one edge then bind off knitwise. Do the same along the second edge.

18 BUTTERFLY BLOOM
Intermediate

A symmetrical daisy is given a ruff of looped stamens, and for fun a three-dimensional garter stitch butterfly has been attached. Both flower and butterfly could be made in varying colorways.

METHOD

Yarn DK wool in sky blue (A), soft orange (B), yellow (C), brown (D), black (E), and white (F).

Equipment 2 pairs of knitting needles, one a size smaller than the other.

FLOWER BLOCK
Using larger needles and A, cast on 35 sts by the thumb method (see page 24).
Beginning with a k row, work mainly in st-st from the chart, reading RS rows from right to left and WS rows from left to right, as indicated by row numbering. When 41st row has been completed, bind off knitwise.

To neaten the sides, RS facing and using A, pick up and k35 sts along one edge then bind off knitwise. Do the same along the second edge.

BUTTERFLY
Body and first wing
Using smaller needles and E, cast on 6 sts by knitting-on method (see page 24)
1st row (RS) Bind off 3 sts, k to end. 3 sts.
Change to F.
2nd row P.
3rd row K1, [yo, k1] twice. 5 sts.
4th row K1, [k1tbl, k1] twice.
5th row K1, yo, k3, yo, k1. 7 sts.
6th row K1, k1tbl, k3, k1tbl, k1.
7th row K1, yo, k5, yo, k1. 9 sts.
8th row K1, k1tbl, k5, k1tbl, k1.
9th row K.
10th row K6, turn, wyab slip 1 purlwise, k5.
11th row K3, turn, wyab slip 1 purlwise, k2.
Bind off knitwise.

Second wing
RS facing and using F pick up and k in each of first 3 sts of body.
1st row (WS) P.
2nd row K1, [yo, k1] twice. 5 sts.
3rd row K1, [k1tbl, k1] twice.
4th row K1, yo, k3, yo, k1. 7 sts.
5th row K1, k1tbl, k3, k1tbl, k1.
6th row K1, yo, k5, yo, k1. 9 sts.
7th row K1, k1tbl, k5, k1tbl, k1.
8th row K6, turn, wyab slip 1 purlwise, k5.
9th row K3, turn, wyab slip 1 purlwise, k2.
10th row K.
Bind off knitwise.

Making up Using E, make a French knot on each wing (see page 30). Use E to stitch the butterfly in place, leaving the wings free and making a straight stitch for each antenna.

Stitch Key

☐ k on RS, p on WS

◉ make loop: k1 without slipping st off needle,
bring yarn between needles to the front, take it
clockwise around left thumb and then between
needles to the back, k the same st again, this time
slipping it from needle, drop loop and slip 2 sts
just made on to left-hand needle, k2tog tbl.

Color Key

 A

■ B

■ C

■ D

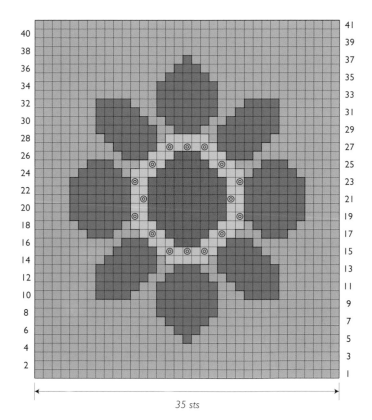

35 sts

19 SUNFLOWER
Intermediate

This sunflower with curly petals has an unusual construction. Its center is garter stitch, with the petals picked up and bound off to make long picots, then eight sections are knitted outward to form an octagon.

METHOD

Yarn DK wool in olive-brown (A), yellow (B), and olive (C).

Equipment A pair of knitting needles and 5 double-pointed knitting needles

CENTER
Using pair of needles and A, cast on 8 sts.
1st row (RS) Kfb, k to last 2 sts, kfb, k1. 10 sts.
2nd row K.
Repeat 1st and 2nd rows 3 times more. 16 sts. Work 8 rows g-st straight.
17th row K1, k2tog, k to last 3 sts, k2tog, k1. 14 sts.
18th row K.
Repeat 17th and 18th rows 3 times more. 8 sts.
Bind off.

PETALS
RS facing, using double-pointed needles and B, distributing 16 sts on each of 4 needles, pick up and k 8 sts from cast-on edge, 8 sts from shaped edge, 8 sts from row ends, 8 sts from shaped edge, 8 sts from bound-off edge, 8 sts from shaped edge, 8 sts from row ends, and 8 sts from shaped edge. 64 sts.
1st round (RS) K. Turn in order to work 2nd round on WS:
2nd round * Cast on 3 sts, bind off 5 sts, slip st from right-hand needle to left-hand needle; repeat from * to end.
Fasten off.

BORDER
* RS facing and folding petals forward, using pair of needles and C, pick up and k one st in back loop of each of 8 sts of one group in 1st petal round, turn.
1st, 2nd, and 3rd rows K.
4th row (RS) Kfb, k5, kfb, k1. 10 sts.
5th, 6th, 7th, and 8th rows K.
Bind off knitwise.
Repeat from * 7 times.

Making up RS together, backstitich pairs of row ends to complete the border. Lightly press the center to a circle. On WS, press the seams of border.

20 STAR FLOWER
Intermediate

Squares knitted from corner to corner become raised, diamond-shaped petals when five are joined together. Add stamens to create a star-shaped flower resting on a garter-stitch background.

METHOD

Yarn Sport weight wool in purple (A), mauve (B), acid yellow (C), and dull lime green (D)

Equipment A pair of knitting needles and crochet hook or wool needle

Specific abbreviations
mb make bobble: [insert hook in last ch, yrh, pull loop through, 1ch] twice, yrh, pull yarn through all loops on hook, fasten off; **ybk** take yarn to back of work; **yfwd** bring yarn forward to front of work

PETALS (make 5)
Using A, cast on 25 sts by thumb method (see page 24).
1st row (RS) K11, s2kpo, k11. 23 sts.
2nd row K11, yfwd, slip 1 purlwise, ybk, k11.
3rd row K10, s2kpo, k10. 21 sts.
4th and WS rows K to center st, yfwd, slip 1 purlwise, ybk, k to end.
5th row K9, s2kpo, k9. 19 sts.
7th row K8, s2kpo, k8. 17 sts.
9th row K7, s2kpo, k7. 15 sts.
11th row K6, s2kpo, k6. 13 sts.
13th row K5, s2kpo, k5. 11 sts.
14th row As 4th row.
Change to B.
15th row K4, s2kpo, k4. 9 sts.
17th row K3, s2kpo, k3. 7 sts.
19th row K2, s2kpo, k2. 5 sts.
21st row K1, s2kpo, k1. 3 sts.
23rd row S2kpo.
Fasten off remaining one st.

BLOCK
Using D, cast on 43 sts. Work 85 rows g-st, or until the block is square (see page 32). Bind off knitwise.

Making up RS together and using yarn ends, backstitch petals, color B to the center. Starting at the center, RS facing, use crochet hook and C to make a surface chain (see page 30) to halfway along one seam, ending by breaking the yarn, leaving a long end and pulling this through to RS. Mb then take yarn to WS. Alternatively, use wool needle to make chain st and end with a large French knot (see page 30). Do the same along remaining seams. Use A to attach the flower to the block, leaving cast-on edges of petals free.

21 **BOBBLE BOUQUET**
Intermediate

This little bunch of flowers with its ribbon bow could be made in any color scheme, according to yarn and ribbon availability. The flower stems are simply twist stitches and two eyelet holes are made to slot the ribbon through.

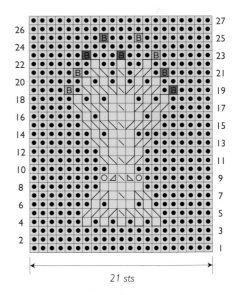

Stitch Key

☐ k on RS, p on WS

● p on RS, k on WS

◣ k1tbl

O yarn over needle

B make bobble: take A to the back, then, using contrast color indicated, (k1, yo, k1) in one st, turn, k1, [yo, k1] twice to make 5 sts, turn, p5, turn, k5, turn, pass 2nd, 3rd, 4th and 5th sts over first st, then, using A, k this st tbl, break contrast yarn and bring A to the front.

◲ ssk

◿ k2tog

◥◥ t2L

◿◿ t2R

Color Key

▨ A

■ B

▨ C

▨ D

■ E

■ F

METHOD

Yarn DK wool in pale green (A), shocking pink (B), pale pink (C), lilac (D), mauve (E), and plum (F)

Equipment A pair of knitting needles, ribbon approximately 12in (30cm) long

Using A, cast on 21 sts by the thumb method (see page 24). Beginning with a p row, work 3 rows reverse st-st. Now continue from the 4th row of the chart, noting that this is a WS row. Read WS rows from left

to right and RS rows from right to left, as indicated by the row numbering. When 27th row has been completed, bind off knitwise. To neaten the edges, RS facing and using A, pick up and k21 sts along one edge then bind off knitwise. Do the same along the second edge.

Making up Press reverse st-st only. Thread the ribbon through the eyelet holes on 9th row, tie a bow, and trim the ends.

21 sts

22 70'S DAISY
Advanced

This is a real flower-power design made using appliqué and fairly straightforward knitting techniques. The center of the daisy is striped with turning rows, and the petals are knitted in a continuous strip.

METHOD

Yarn DK wool in pea green (A), yellow-green (B), cream (C), and deep turquoise (D)

Equipment A pair of knitting needles

CENTER
Using A, cast on 9 sts by the thumb method (see page 24).
Note Do not break yarn between colors.
1st row (RS) Using B, k7, turn, wyab slip 1 purlwise, k6.
2nd row (RS) K5, turn, wyab slip 1 purlwise, k4.
3rd row (RS) Using A, k all 9 sts.
4th row (WS) Slip 1 knitwise, k to end.
Repeat 1st–4th rows 14 times more, then work 1st and 2nd rows again.
Using A, bind off knitwise.

PETALS
Using C, cast on 4 sts.
Note Slip all slip stitches knitwise.
1st row (RS) Slip 1, kfb, k2. 5 sts.
2nd row Slip 1, k2, kfb, k1. 6 sts.
3rd row Slip 1, kfb, k4. 7 sts.
4th row Slip 1, k4, kfb, k1. 8 sts.
5th, 6th, 7th, and 8th rows Slip 1, k7.
9th row Slip 1, k2tog, k5. 7 sts.
10th row Slip 1, k3, k2tog, k1. 6 sts.
11th row Slip 1, k2tog, k3. 5 sts.
12th row Slip 1, k1, k2tog, k1. 4 sts.
13th row Slipping first st, bind off 2 sts, k remaining one st. 2 sts.
14th row Slip 1, k1, turn, cast on 2 sts by knitting-on method (see page 24). 4 sts.
Do not turn.
Repeat 1st–14th rows 7 times more, then work 1st–13th rows again.
Bind off remaining 2 sts.

BLOCK
Using D, cast on 31 sts.
1st row (RS) K1, [p1, k1] 15 times.
2nd row As 1st row. Repeat these 2 rows until 51 rows have been completed or until block is square (see page 32).
Bind off knitwise.
To neaten the sides, RS facing and using D, pick up and k31 sts along one edge, then bind off knitwise. Do the same along the second edge.

Making up Seam the center, using A and taking in the chain edge of the bind off and the single back strand of the cast on. Gently stretch the outer edge and gather the inner edge tightly. Seam the petals by joining the 2 bound-off stitches and the inner 2 cast-on stitches. Attach the center to the block by over-sewing the outer edge. Set the petals on top and, using C, back stitch on RS around slip stitch edge. Press the nose of the iron into each petal to make it concave.

23 POPPY
Intermediate

For a very open effect, six-petal flowers can be assembled like hexagons or, more conventionally, they could be mounted on square blocks. This poppy is made as a strip of petals with the center picked up and knitted before being joined into a ring.

METHOD

Yarn Sport-weight wool in scarlet (A) and black (B)

Equipment A pair of knitting needles

Specific stitch
loop 1 k1 without slipping st off needle, bring yarn between needles to the front, take it clockwise around left thumb and then between needles to the back, k the same st again this time slipping it from needle, drop loop and slip 2 sts just made on to left-hand needle, k2tog tbl.

Note Each time a turn is made mid-row the wrap-and-turn technique should be used to prevent a hole: before turning, take the yarn to the opposite side of the work, slip the next stitch purlwise from the left-hand needle to the right-hand needle, return the yarn to the original side of the work, slip the stitch back on to the left-hand needle, turn, tension the yarn ready to work the next stitch.

PETALS
Using A, cast on 10 sts by the cable method (see page 24).
1st row (RS) Kfb, k8, turn, p to end. 11 sts.
2nd row (RS) As 1st row. 12 sts.
3rd and 5th rows K.
4th and 6th rows P.
7th row Ssk, k9, turn, p to end.
8th row Ssk, k7, turn, p to end. 10 sts.
9th row Slipping first st knitwise, bind off 4 sts, k to end. 6 sts.
10th row P, turn, cast on 4 sts by cable method. 10 sts.
Repeat 1st–10th rows 4 times more, then work 1st–9th rows again.
Bind off purlwise.

CENTER
RS facing and using A, pick up and k6 sts from the inside edge of each petal. 36 sts.
Change to B.
1st row P.
2nd row K1, [loop 1] 34 times, k1.
3rd row [K4, k2tog] 6 times. 30 sts.
4th row [K3, k2tog] 6 times. 24 sts.

5th row [K2, k2tog] 6 times. 18 sts.
6th row [K1, k2tog] 6 times. 12 sts.
7th row [K2tog] 6 times. 6 sts.
Break yarn, leaving a long yarn end, and thread this through sts.

Making up Pull yarn end B to gather the center, then use it to seam the row ends of the center. Join the 6 sts of bind off of the last petal to inner 6 sts of cast on of the first petal.
Press petals to shape.

24 CROCUS
Intermediate

The increases that make this flower so heavily embossed mean that the stitch count is not the same on every row. But this doesn't make it particularly difficult to knit.

METHOD

Yarn DK cotton

Equipment A pair of knitting needles

Cast on 27 sts by the thumb method (see page 24).
1st row (RS) P.
2nd row K.
Repeat 1st and 2nd rows 3 times more.
9th row P13, k1, p13.
10th row K13, p1, k13.
11th row P12, k3, p12.
12th row K12, p3, k12.
13th row P11, k2tog, yo, k1, yo, skpo, p11.
14th row K11, p5, k11.
15th row P10, k2tog, k1, [yo] twice, k1, [yo] twice, k1, skpo, p10. 29 sts.
16th row K10, p2, (k1, p1) in double yo, p1, (p1, k1) in double yo, p2, k10.
17th row P9, k2tog, k2, yo, k1, [yo] twice, k1, [yo] twice, k1, yo, k2, skpo, p9. 33 sts.
18th row K9, p5, [k1, p1] in double yo, p1, [p1, k1] in double yo, p5, k9.
19th row P8, k2tog, k5, yo, [k1, yo] 3 times, k5, skpo, p8. 35 sts.
20th and 22nd rows K8, p19, k8.
21st row P8, k19, p8.

23rd row P8, k5, yo, skpo, k5, k2tog, yo, k5, p8.
24th row K8, p5, k1tbl, p7, k1tbl, p5, k8.
25th row P8, k2, k2sso, yo, p1, yo, skpo, k3, k2tog, yo, p1, yo, sk2po, k2, p8. 33 sts.
26th row K8, p3, k1tbl, k1, k1tbl, p5, k1tbl, k1, k1tbl, p3, k8.
27th row P8, k2sso, p3, yo, skpo, k1, k2tog, yo, p3, sk2po, p8. 29 sts.
28th row K12, k1tbl, p3, k1tbl, k12.
29th row P13, s2kpo, p13. 27 sts.
30th row K13, p1, k13.
Beginning with a p row, work 6 rows reverse st-st to complete 36 rows.
Bind off purlwise.

To neaten the sides, RS facing, pick up and k27 sts along one edge then bind off knitwise. Do the same along the second edge.

25   FORMAL FLOWER
Intermediate

Eight bobbles form a flower head that is set between two embossed leaves. This design forms one of the trio that includes Crocus (page 61) and Spring Bulb (page 63).

METHOD

Yarn DK cotton

Equipment A pair of knitting needles and a cable needle

Specific abbreviations
c3bp slip next 2 sts on to cable needle and hold at back, k1 then p2 from cable needle;
c3fp slip next st on to cable needle and hold at front, p2 then k1 from cable needle;
mb make bobble: [k1, p1, k1, p1, k1] in one st, turn, p5, turn, pass 2nd, 3rd, 4th, and 5th sts over first st, k this st tbl.

Cast on 27 sts.
1st row (RS) P.
2nd row K.
Repeat 1st and 2nd rows 3 times more.
9th row P12, k3, p12.
10th row K12, p3, k12.
11th row P10, c3bp, k1, c3fp, p10.
12th row K10, p1, [k2, p1] twice, k10.
13th row P8, c3bp, p2, k1, p2, c3fp, p8.
14th row K8, p1, [k4, p1] twice, k8.
15th row P8, yo, k1, yo, p4, k1, p4, yo, k1, yo, p8. 31 sts.
16th row K8, p3, k4, p1, k4, p3, k8.

17th row P8, k1, [yo, k1] twice, [p4, k1] twice, [yo, k1] twice, p8. 35 sts.
18th row K8, p5, k4, p1, k4, p5, k8.
19th row P8, k2, yo, k1, yo, k2, p4, k1, p4, k2, yo, k1, yo, k2, p8. 39 sts.
20th row K8, p7, k4, p1, k4, p7, k8.
21st row P8, k5, k2tog, p4, k1, p4, skpo, k5, p8. 37 sts.
22nd row K8, p6, k4, p1, k4, p6, k8.
23rd row P8, k4, k2tog, p3, mb, k1, mb, p3, skpo, k4, p8. 35 sts.
24th row K8, p5, k3, p3, k3, p5, k8.
25th row P8, k2, k2sso, p2, mb, k3, mb, p2, sk2po, k2, p8. 31 sts.
26th row K8, p3, k2, p5, k2, p3, k8.
27th row P8, k2sso, p2, mb, k3, mb, p2, sk2po, p8. 27 sts.
28th row K8, p1, k2, p5, k2, p1, k8.
29th row P12, mb, k1, mb, p12.
Beginning with a k row, work 7 rows reverse st-st to complete 36 rows.
Bind off purlwise.
To neaten sides, RS facing, pick up and k27 sts along one edge then bind off knitwise. Do the same along the second edge.

Mix and Match 24 + 25 + 26

26 SPRING BULB
Beginner

Similar in size to Crocus (page 61), this design is different in that it maintains the same stitch count throughout and so is easily followed from a chart. It incorporates two simple cables for additional surface interest.

Stitch Key

☐ k on RS, p on WS

⬛ p on RS, k on WS

Ⓞ yarn over needle

◿ k2tog

◺ skpo

⬛ s2kpo

⬊ k1tbl (WS)

╱ ╱ c3b: slip next st onto cable needle and hold at back, k2 then k1 from cable needle

╲ ╲ c3f: slip next 2 sts onto cable needle and hold at front, k1 then k2 from cable needle

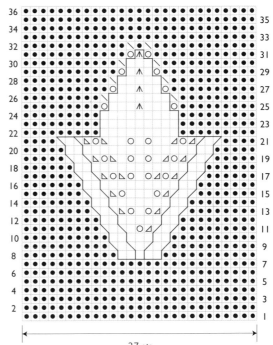

METHOD

Yarn DK cotton

Equipment A pair of knitting needles and a cable needle

Cast on 27 sts by the thumb method (see page 24). Beginning with a p row, work 7 rows reverse st-st. Now continue from 8th row of the chart, noting that this is a WS row. Read WS rows from left to right and RS rows from right to left, as indicated by the row numbering.

When 36th row has been completed, bind off purlwise. To neaten the sides, RS facing, pick up and k27 sts along one edge then bind off knitwise. Do the same along the second edge.

27 sts

27 CORD FLOWER
Beginner

Making a cord with two double-pointed needles is even easier than with the traditional method of French knitting. But either method can be used to make a free-form flower applied to a corner-to-corner block.

METHOD

Yarn DK wool in purple (A), sport-weight wool in shocking pink (B)

Equipment A pair of knitting needles and 2 double-pointed knitting needles

BLOCK

Using pair of needles and A, cast on 2 sts.
1st row (RS) Kfb, k1. 3 sts.
2nd and WS rows K.
3rd row [Kfb] twice, k1. 5 sts.
5th row Kfb, k2, kfb, k1. 7 sts.
7th row Kfb, k4, kfb, k1. 9 sts.
9th row Kfb, k6, kfb, k1. 11 sts.
Continue to increase in this way on RS rows until there are 43 sts.
Next RS row K1, k2tog, k to last 3 sts, k2tog, k1. 41 sts.
Continue to decrease in this way on RS rows until 7 sts remain.
Next RS row K1, [k2tog, k1] twice. 5 sts.
Next RS row K1, sk2po, k1. 3 sts.
Next RS row Sk2po.
Fasten off remaining one st.

CORD

Using 2 double-pointed needles and B, cast on 5 sts.
Knit one row in the usual way.
* Without turning, slide the stitches to the opposite end of the needle. Take the yarn firmly across the wrong side from left to right and knit one row.
Repeat from * until the cord measures approximately 33in (84cm) or required length. Do not bind off but break the yarn, leaving an end long enough to sew with. Join the cord into a ring by grafting the loop of each stitch to a stitch of the cast on.

Making up Square up the block and press lightly. Hiding the join in a curve, pin the cord in position on the block and then baste it, using sport-weight yarn (this will grip better than smooth sewing thread). Making small stitches on the underside of the cord, use B to sew the cord in place.

28 CORD LEAF
Beginner

This graphic leaf can be made just as freely as the Cord Flower (page 64) and is, perhaps, a little easier since the cord doesn't need to be joined.

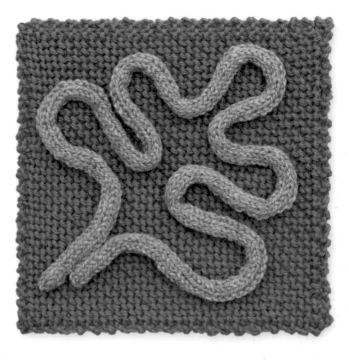

METHOD

Yarn DK wool in blue-green (A), sport-weight wool in apple green (B)

Equipment A pair of knitting needles and 2 double-pointed knitting needles

BLOCK
Using a pair of needles and A, cast on 2 sts.
1st row (RS) Kfb, k1. 3 sts.
2nd and WS rows K.
3rd row [Kfb] twice, k1. 5 sts.
5th row Kfb, k2, kfb, k1. 7 sts.
7th row Kfb, k4, kfb, k1. 9 sts.
9th row Kfb, k6, kfb, k1. 11 sts.
Continue to increase in this way on RS rows until there are 43 sts.
Next RS row K1, k2tog, k to last 3 sts, k2tog, k1. 41 sts.
Continue to decrease in this way on RS rows until 7 sts remain.
Next RS row K1, [k2tog, k1] twice. 5 sts.
Next RS row K1, sk2po, k1. 3 sts.
Next RS row Sk2po.
Fasten off remaining one st.

CORD
Using 2 double-pointed needles and B, cast on 5 sts.
Knit one row in the usual way.
* Without turning, slide the stitches to the opposite end of the needle. Take the yarn firmly across the wrong side from left to right and knit one row.
Repeat from * until cord measures approximately 30in (76cm).
Bind off.

Making up Square up the block and press lightly. Pin the cord in position on the block and then baste it, using sport-weight yarn (this will grip better than smooth sewing thread). Making small stitches on the underside of the cord, use B to sew the cord in place.

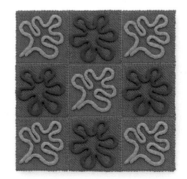

Mix and Match 27 + 28

29 MAPLE LEAF
Advanced

Gigantic eyelets are a decorative feature of this well-defined leaf. Sewing it to its stockinette stitch background needs to be done neatly, but using backstitch on the surface is relatively easy and keeps the outline sharp.

METHOD

Yarn Sport-weight cotton in pale green (A) and dull green (B)

Equipment A pair of knitting needles

STEM
Using A, cast on 3 sts.
1st row (RS) K1, slip 1 purlwise, k1.
2nd row P.
Repeat 1st and 2nd rows 4 times more. Do not break yarn and continue.

LEAF
1st row (RS) Cast on 3 sts by the knitting-on method (see page 24), k4, slip 1 purlwise, k1. 6 sts.
2nd row Cast on 3 sts as before, p9. 9 sts.
3rd row K2, k2tog, [yo] 4 times, k1, [yo] 4 times, ssk, k2.
4th row P3, (k1, yo, k1, yo, k1, yo, k1) in multiple yo, p1, (k1, yo, k1, yo, k1, yo, k1) in multiple yo, p3. 21 sts.
5th row K8, k2tog, [yo] 3 times, k1, [yo] 3 times, ssk, k8.
6th row P9, (k1, yo, k1, yo, k1) in multiple yo, p1, (k1, yo, k1, yo, k1) in multiple yo, p9. 29 sts.
7th row K12, k2tog, [yo] twice, k1, [yo] twice, ssk, k12.

8th row P13, (k1, yo, k1) in double yo, p1, (k1, yo, k1) in double yo, p13. 33 sts.
9th row K14, k2tog, yo, k1, yo, ssk, k14.
10th, 12th, 14th, 16th, and 18th rows P.
11th, 13th, 15th, and 17th rows K.
* **19th row** Ssk, k7, k2tog, turn.
9 sts. Continue on these sts only.
20th, 22nd, 24th, and 26th rows P.
21st row Ssk, k5, k2tog. 7 sts.
23rd row Ssk, k3, k2tog. 5 sts.
25th row Ssk, k1, k2tog. 3 sts.
27th row Sk2po.
Fasten off remaining one st.
RS facing, rejoin yarn to remaining sts and work from * twice more.

BLOCK
Using B, cast on 42 sts. Beginning with a k row, work 51 rows st-st, or until block is square (see page 32).
Bind off knitwise.
To neaten the sides, RS facing and using B, pick up and k42 sts along one edge then bind off knitwise. Do the same along the second edge.

Making up Press to shape. Pin, then baste the leaf to the block. Using A, backstitch around edges of leaf one stitch in from the edge. Catch down center stitches of stem.

30 CLEMATIS
Advanced

Apart from being knitted in the round to avoid a seam, this bold flower is otherwise similar in technique to the Maple Leaf (page 66). Very large eyelets surround the center, one for each of the sharply defined petals.

METHOD

Yarn Sport-weight cotton in pale mauve (A) and deep lilac (B)

Equipment 4 double-pointed knitting needles and a pair of knitting needles

FLOWER
Using double-pointed needles and A, cast on 2 sts on each of 3 needles. 6 sts.
1st round K.
2nd round [Yo, k1] 6 times. 12 sts.
3rd and 5th rounds K.
4th round [Yo, k1] 12 times. 24 sts.
6th round [Yo, k3, yo, k1] 6 times. 36 sts.
7th and 8th rounds K.
9th round * K1, k2tog, [yo] 4 times, skpo, k1; repeat from * 5 times more. 48 sts.
10th round [K2, (k1, yo, k1, yo, k1, yo, k1) in multiple yo, k2] 6 times. 66 sts.
11th and 12th rounds K.
** **13th round** Ssk, k7, k2tog, turn. 9 sts. Continue in rows on these sts only.
14th, 16th, 18th, and 20th rows P.

15th row Ssk, k5, k2tog. 7 sts.
17th row Ssk, k3, k2tog. 5 sts.
19th row Ssk, k1, k2tog. 3 sts.
21st row Sk2po.
Fasten off remaining one st.
RS facing, rejoin yarn to remaining sts and repeat from ** 5 times more.

BLOCK
Using B and pair of knitting needles, cast on 42 sts. Beginning with a k row, work 51 rows st-st, or until block is square (see page 32). Bind off knitwise.
To neaten the sides, RS facing and using B, pick up and k42 sts along one edge then bind off knitwise. Do the same along the second edge.

Making up Press to shape. Pin and baste the flower in position on the block. Using A, backstitch around edge of the flower, one stitch in from the edge.

Mix and Match 29 + 30

31 BOBBLE BLOSSOM
Advanced

Vibrant color adds to the impact of a raised bobble-and-leaf design. Because of the variety of cables involved, the instructions are given as a chart.

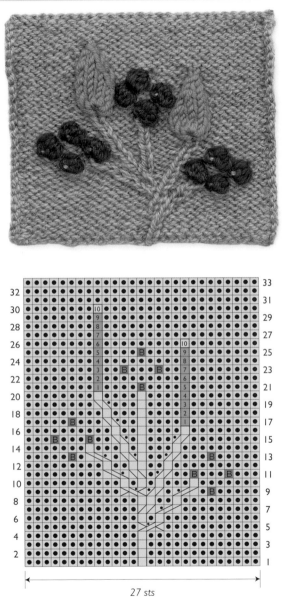

Stitch Key

☐ k on RS, p on WS

● p on RS, k on WS

⊿ k2tog

◺ skpo

◹ k2sso

◸ sk2po

✳ p1A (WS)

○ yarn over needle

// c2b

\\ c2f

•// c2bp

\\• c2fp

⤬ slip 2 sts onto cable needle and hold at back, k1 then p1, k1 from cable needle

⤬ slip one st onto cable needle and hold at front, k1, p1 then k1 from cable needle

•⟋ slip 2 sts onto cable needle and hold at back, k1 then p2 from cable needle

⟍• slip one st onto cable needle and hold at front, p2 then k1 from cable needle

B̲ make bobble: using B, (k1, yo, k1, yo, k1) in one st, turn, p5, turn, pass 2nd, 3rd, 4th and 5th sts over first st, then, using A, k this st tbl

Color Key

■ A

■ B

■ C

METHOD

Yarn Sport-weight wool in lime green (A), fuchsia (B), and bright green (C)

Equipment A pair of knitting needles and a cable needle

Using A, cast on 27 sts by the thumb method (see page 24). Now pattern from the chart, reading RS rows from right to left and WS rows from left to right, as indicated by the row numbering.

Note On 17th row begin Leaf 1 shown on the right-hand side of the main chart and on 21st row begin Leaf 2 shown on the left-hand side of the chart. The first row of each leaf is worked (k1, yo, k1, yo, k1) in one st. The st count is then as shown on the charts.

27 sts

Note that the last st of each supplementary chart is p1A on WS.

When 33rd row has been completed, bind off knitwise. To neaten the sides, RS facing and using A, pick up and k27 sts along one edge then bind off knitwise. Do the same along second edge.

32 FLOWER GARDEN
Intermediate

Varying the colors of the groups of bobbles turns a regular repeat pattern into a lively flower garden. Here shades of blue have been used but a mixture of colors would give an even brighter effect.

Stitch Key

☐ k on RS, p on WS

O yarn over needle

⊿ k2tog

⊾ skpo

B make bobble: using contrast color, (k1, p1, k1) in one st, turn, p3, turn, using A, sk2po

Color Key

▨ A

▨ B

▨ C

▨ D

▨ E

▨ F

METHOD

Yarn DK wool in lime green (A), bright blue (B), sky blue (C), royal blue (D), pale blue (E), and periwinkle (F)

Equipment A pair of knitting needles

Using A, cast on 31 sts by the thumb method (see page 24). Beginning with a k row, work 4 rows st-st. Now continue from 5th row of the chart, reading RS rows from right to left and WS rows from left to right, as indicated by the row numbering. When 37th row has been completed, bind off knitwise.

To neaten the sides, RS facing and using A, pick up and k31 sts along one edge then bind off knitwise. Do the same along the second edge.

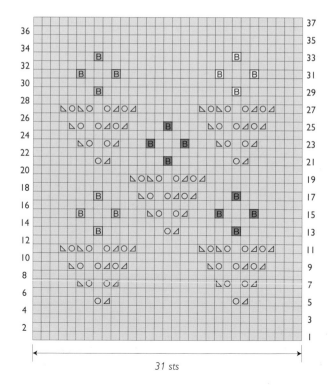

31 sts

33 DAISY
Intermediate

This appliqué daisy is made all the chunkier by being stitched to a garter-stitch background. The design is deliberately not dainty—it's children's coloring book in style.

METHOD

Yarn DK wool in sap green (A), soft white (B), candy pink (C), and teal (D)

Equipment A pair of knitting needles

Specific abbreviation
pfkb p in front then k in back of st

STEM
Using A, cast on 3 sts. Beginning with a k row, work 18 rows st-st. Do not break yarn and continue.

FLOWER
1st row (RS) [Kfb] twice, k1. 5 sts.
2nd row [Pfkb] 4 times, p1. 9 sts.
3rd row [K1, p1] 4 times, k1.
4th row [P1, k1] 4 times, p1.
5th row [K1, m1, p1] 4 times, k1. 13 sts.
6th row [P1, k2] 4 times, p1.
7th row [K1, p2] 4 times, k1.
8th row As 6th row.
Change to B.
9th row K.
10th row P.
11th row K2, [m1, k3] 3 times, m1, k2. 17 sts.
12th row P2, [k1, p3] 3 times, k1, p2.
13th row K2, [p1, k3] 3 times, p1, k2.
14th row As 12th row.
Change to C.

15th row K.
16th row P.
17th row [K2tog, yo] 8 times, k1.
18th row P.
Bind off loosely knitwise.
Fold along 17th row to make picots and catch down along color-change row on WS.

BLOCK
Using D, cast on 2 sts.
1st row (RS) Kfb, k1. 3 sts.
2nd and WS rows K.
3rd row [Kfb] twice, k1. 5 sts.
5th row Kfb, k2, kfb, k1. 7 sts.
7th row Kfb, k4, kfb, k1. 9 sts.
9th row Kfb, k6, kfb, k1. 11 sts.
Continue to increase in this way on RS rows until there are 31 sts.
Next RS row K1, k2tog, k to last 3 sts, k2tog, k1.
Continue to decrease in this way on RS rows until 7 sts remain.
Next RS row K1, [k2tog, k1] twice. 5 sts.
Next RS row K1, sk2po, k1. 3 sts.
Next RS row Sk2po. Fasten off remaining one st.

Making up Square up the block and press lightly. Attach daisy by using matching yarn to over-sew along edges, taking in only the outermost strand of each edge stitch.

Mix and Match 33 + 34

34 SPRING LEAF
Intermediate

This fresh, green leaf can be used with the Daisy design (page 70) or the Lily (page 80). It has twist-stitch veins and sits on a diagonal garter-stitch block.

METHOD

Yarn DK wool in pale green (A) and leaf green (B)

Equipment A pair of knitting needles

STEM
Using A, cast on 3 sts. Beginning with a k row, work 12 rows st-st. Do not break yarn and continue.

LEAF
Note All slip stitches are slipped purlwise.
1st row (RS) K1, slip 1, k1.
2nd row K1, p1, k1.
3rd row K1, m1R, slip 1, m1L, k1. 5 sts.
4th row K1, p3, k1.
5th row K1, m1R, k1, slip 1, k1, m1L, k1. 7 sts.
6th and WS rows K1, p to last st, k1.
7th row K1, m1R, t2R, slip 1, t2L, m1L, k1. 9 sts.
9th row K1, m1R, t2R, k1, slip 1, k1, t2L, m1L, k1. 11 sts.
11th row K1, m1R, [t2R] twice, slip 1, [t2L] twice, m1L, k1. 13 sts.
13th row K1, m1R, [t2R] twice, k1, slip 1, k1, [t2L] twice, m1L, k1. 15 sts.
15th row K1, m1R, [t2R] 3 times, slip 1, [t2L] 3 times, m1L, k1. 17 sts.
17th row K1, [t2R] 3 times, k1, slip 1, k1, [t2L] 3 times, k1.
19th row K2, [t2R] 3 times, slip 1, [t2L] 3 times, k2.
21st row As 17th row.
23rd row As 19th row.
25th row K1, k2tog, [t2R] twice, k1, slip 1, k1, [t2L] twice, ssk, k1. 15 sts.
27th row K1, k2tog, [t2R] twice, slip 1, [t2L] twice, ssk, k1. 13 sts.
29th row K3tog, t2R, k1, slip 1, k1, t2L, sk2po. 9 sts.
31st row K3tog, s2kpo, sk2po. 3 sts.
32nd row K1, p1, k1.
33rd row S2kpo.
Fasten off remaining one st.

BLOCK
Using B, cast on 2 sts.
1st row (RS) Kfb, k1. 3 sts.
2nd and WS rows K.
3rd row [Kfb] twice, k1. 5 sts.
5th row Kfb, k2, kfb, k1. 7 sts.
7th row Kfb, k4, kfb, k1. 9 sts
9th row Kfb, k6, kfb, k1. 11 sts.
Continue to increase in this way on RS rows until there are 31 sts.
Next RS row K1, k2tog, k to last 3 sts, k2tog, k1.

Continue to decrease in this way on RS rows until 7 sts remain.
Next RS row K1, [k2tog, k1] twice. 5 sts.
Next RS row K1, sk2po, k1. 3 sts.
Next RS row Sk2po.
Fasten off remaining one st.

Making up Square up the block and press lightly. Using A, backstitch the leaf in place on RS, one stitch in from the edge stitch. Catch down the edge stitches of the stem.

35 BLUE LEAF
Advanced

The shape of the leaf is made with twist stitches and stockinette stitch on a reverse stockinette stitch background. This is then outlined with a length of picot hem, making it a partner for Marigold (page 73).

METHOD

Yarn Worsted-weight wool

Equipment A pair of knitting needles

Specific abbreviation
t2Rp k in 2nd st on left-hand needle, p in first st, slip both sts off together.

BLOCK
Cast on 17 sts by the thumb method (see page 24).
1st, 3rd, and 5th rows P.
2nd and 4th rows K.
6th row (WS) K4, p7, k6.
7th row P6, t2R, k3, t2R,p4.
8th row K4, p8, k5.
9th row P5, t2R, k3, t2R, k1, p4.
10th row K4, p9, k4.
11th row P4, t2R, k3, t2R, k2, p4.
12th row As 10th row.
13th row P4, k4, t2R, k1, t2Rp, p4.
14th row K5, p8, k4.
15th row P4, k6, t2Rp, p5.
16th row K6, p7, k4.
17th row P4, k5, t2Rp, p6.

18th and 20th rows K.
19th and 21st rows P.
22nd row K.
Bind off purlwise.

PICOT EDGING
Leaving a long end for sewing, cast on 37 sts.
1st row (WS) P18, m1, p1, m1, p18. 39 sts.
2nd row [K2tog, yo] 19 times, k1.
3rd row P18, p3tog, p18. 37 sts.
4th row Form picots by folding widthwise along 2nd row, then join by binding off knitwise each stitch on the needle together with a single strand of each corresponding stitch of the cast-on edge.

Making up Take the second yarn end under the first chain of the bound-off edge and back again (see page 27), use this end to join the picots into a ring. Position this join at the base of the leaf, pinch the point at the top and use the first yarn end to sew the picots around the outline of the leaf, making a backstitch underneath alternate chains of the bound-off edge.
To neaten the sides, RS facing, pick up and k17 sts along one edge, then bind off knitwise. Do the same along the second edge.

36 MARIGOLD
Advanced

Clever cabling outlines the center of this chunky flower. The petals are a length of picot added afterward. A few sewing skills are needed to do this neatly, but it's not too difficult.

METHOD

Yarn Worsted-weight wool

Equipment A pair of knitting needles and a cable needle

Specific abbreviations

c3bp slip one st on to cable needle and hold at back, k2 then p1 from cable needle.

c3fp slip 2 sts on to cable needle and hold at front, p1 then k2 from cable needle.

c4bp slip 2 sts on to cable needle and hold at back, k2 then p2 from cable needle.

c4fp slip 2 sts on to cable needle and hold at front, p2 then k2 from cable needle.

dec 4 leaving yarn at back, slip 3 sts purlwise, * on right-hand needle pass 2nd st over first, slip this st back on to left-hand needle, pass next st over it, ** slip this st back on to right-hand needle then repeat from * to ** once more to leave one st on left-hand needle, k this st tbl.

d inc make 3 sts from one: [k1tbl, k1] in next st, insert point of left-hand needle behind vertical strand between 2 sts just made and k in back of this strand.

BLOCK
Cast on 17 sts by thumb method (see page 24).
1st row (RS) P.
2nd row K.
Repeat 1st and 2nd rows twice more.
7th row P8, m1, d inc, m1, p8. 21 sts.
8th row K8, p2, k1, p2, k8.
9th row P6, c4bp, p1, c4fp, p6.
10th row K6, p2, k5, p2, k6.
11th row P5, c3bp, p5, c3fp, p5.
12th row K5, p2, k7, p2, k5.
13th row P5, k2, p7, k2, p5.
14th row As 12th row.
15th row P5, c3fp, p5, c3bp, p5.
16th row As 10th row.
17th row P6, c4fp, p1, c4bp, p6.
18th row K8, dec 4, k8. 17 sts.
19th and 21st rows P.
20th and 22nd rows K.
Bind off purlwise.

PICOT PETALS
Leaving a long end for sewing, cast on 31 sts.
1st row (WS) P.
2nd row [K2tog, yo] 15 times, k1.
3rd row P.
4th row Form picots by folding widthwise along 2nd row, then join by binding off knitwise each stitch on the needle together with a single strand of each corresponding stitch of the cast-on edge. Fasten off leaving a long end.

Making up Take the second yarn end under the first chain of the bound-off edge and back again (see page 27), use this end to join the petals into a ring. Use the first yarn end to sew the petal ring around the cabled ring, making a backstitch underneath alternate chains of the bound-off edge. To neaten the sides, RS facing, pick up and k17 sts along side edge, then bind off knitwise. Do the same along the second edge.

37 WINDOW BOX
Intermediate

Threesomes of bobbles in purples and mauves suggest little pansies but, of course, a different color scheme could be used. These bobbles are worked over two rows without the usual turning rows.

Stitch Key

☐ k on RS, p on WS

● p on RS

⁄⁄ t2R

V (k1, yo, k1, yo, k1) in st to make 5 sts from one

∧ k5 then pass 2nd, 3rd, 4th, and 5th sts over first st

Color Key

■ A

■ B

■ C

■ D

■ E

■ F

METHOD

Yarn DK wool in lime (A), olive (B), pink-mauve (C), aubergine (D), mauve (E), and plum (F)

Equipment A pair of knitting needles

Note Use the intarsia color change technique for the window box (see page 26) and the stranding technique for the bobbles (see page 26).

Using A, cast on 29 sts by the thumb method (see page 24). Beginning with a k row, work 5 rows st-st. Now continue from 6th row of the chart, noting that this is a WS row, reading WS rows from left to right and RS rows from right to left, as indicated by the row numbering. When 33rd row has been completed bind off knitwise.

To neaten the sides, RS facing and using A, pick up and k29 sts along one edge then bind off knitwise. Do the same along the second edge.

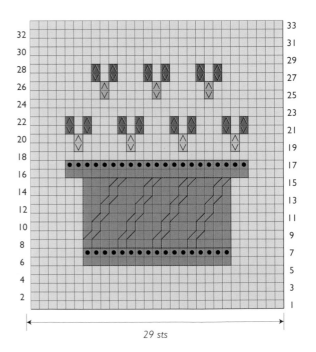

29 sts

38 DAISY MEADOW
Beginner

Twisted rib and a few twist stitches suggest a grassy meadow with knitted daisies added randomly.

Stitch Key

☐ k1tbl on RS, p1tbl on WS

● p1 on RS, k1 on WS

⁄⁄ t2R

⁄⁄ t2Rp: k in front of 2nd st, then p in front of first st, slip both sts off needle together

METHOD

Yarn Sport-weight wool in grass green (A), yellow (B), and soft white (C)

Equipment A pair of knitting needles

BLOCK

Using A, cast on 33 sts.
1st row (RS) P1, [k1tbl, p1] 16 times.
2nd row K1, [p1tbl, k1] 16 times.
Repeat 1st and 2nd rows 3 times more.
Now work from chart, reading RS rows from right to left and WS rows from left to right, as indicated by the row numbering. When 16th row of chart has been completed work 10 rows twisted rib.
Bind off in rib.

DAISIES (make 3)

Using B, cast on 4 sts by the thumb method (see page 24).
1st row (RS) K1, [yo, k1] 3 times. 7 sts.
2nd row K1, [k1tbl, k1] 3 times. Change to C.
3rd row K.
4th row * Cast on 3 sts by cable method (see page 24), bind off 4 sts knitwise, slip remaining st from right-hand needle to left-hand needle; repeat from * 5 times. Fasten off remaining one st.

HALF DAISIES (make 2)

Using C, cast on 5 sts.
1st row (RS) K.
2nd row * Cast on 3 sts, bind off 4 sts, slip remaining st from right-hand needle to left-hand needle; repeat from * 3 times. Fasten off remaining one st.

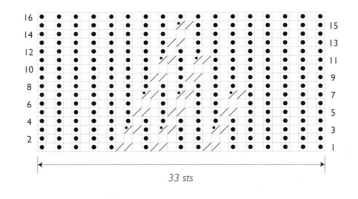

33 sts

Making up

Daisies: Use first yarn end B to gather the cast-on edge tightly, then join the row ends.
Half daisies: Use first yarn end C to gather slightly the cast-on edge. Stitch all the flowers in place on the block, leaving the petals free.

39 CORSAGE
Intermediate

Some basic crochet skills and very basic knitting skills are needed to make this design. In fact, it's a familiar Irish rose except that the petals are knitted in garter stitch. For piecing, the outer petals can be joined for an open effect or the flower could be set on a block for a more substantial result.

METHOD

Yarn DK wool in magenta (A) and blue-pink (B)

Equipment A pair of knitting needles and a crochet hook

CENTER
Using crochet hook and A, make a slip ring (see page 25).
Working in a round with RS facing, make 2ch, into ring make 7sc, pull yarn end to close ring, join with ss in top ch of 2ch. 8 sts.
2nd round 1ch, [5ch, miss 1sc, 1sc in next sc] 4 times, ending ss in first ch. 4 ch loops.
Fasten off.

INNER PETALS
RS facing and using A, in one loop: * insert hook under ch, yrh, pull yarn through, yrh, pull loop through to enclose ch, slip loop from hook on to knitting needle; in same ch loop repeat from * 8 times. 9 sts on needle. Turn. **
Beginning with a WS row, work 7 rows g-st.
8th row [K2tog] twice, k1, [k2tog] twice. 5 sts.
Bind off knitwise.
Make 3 more petals in the same way.

OUTER PETALS
RS facing, fold a petal forward and, using crochet hook and A, insert the hook in one of the free sc of first round, 1ch, [7ch, fold next petal forward, 1sc in next free sc of first round] 4 times, ending ss in first ch. 4 ch loops.
Fasten off.
RS facing, fold a petal forward in order to work into the ch loop behind and, using crochet hook and B, making 13 sts instead of 9 sts, work as inner petal from * to **. Beginning with a WS row, work 3 rows g-st.
4th row (RS) Kfb, k10, kfb, k1. 15 sts. Work 5 rows g-st.
10th row K2tog, k11, k2tog. 13 sts.
11th row K.
12th row K2tog, k9, k2tog. 11 sts.
Bind off knitwise.
Make 3 more petals in the same way.

40 RIBBED ROSE
Beginner

This is a real beginner's piece as the rose is simply a length of knit two, purl two rib coiled round and sewn to a corner-to-corner garter stitch block.

METHOD

Yarn Sport-weight wool in shocking pink (A), pale pink (B), and green (C)

Equipment A pair of knitting needles

ROSE
Using A and leaving a long yarn end, cast on 94 sts.
1st row K2, [p2, k2] to end.
2nd row P2, [k2, p2] to end.
Change to B. Repeat 1st and 2nd rows twice more, then work 1st row again.
Leaving a long yarn end, bind off loosely in rib.

BLOCK
Using C, cast on 2 sts.
1st row (RS) Kfb, k1. 3 sts.
2nd and WS rows K.
3rd row [Kfb] twice, k1. 5 sts.

5th row Kfb, k2, kfb, k1. 7 sts.
7th row Kfb, k4, kfb, k1. 9 sts.
9th row Kfb, k6, kfb, k1. 11 sts.
Continue to increase in this way on RS rows until there are 27 sts.
Next RS row K1, k2tog, k to last 3 sts, k2tog, k1.
Continue to decrease in this way on RS rows until 7 sts remain.
Next RS row K1, [k2tog, k1] twice. 5 sts.
Next RS row K1, sk2po, k1. 3 sts.
Next RS row Sk2po.
Fasten off remaining one st.

Making up Square up the block and press lightly. Use long yarn end A to gather the cast-on sts of rib. Coil the rib and sew cast-on edge to the block. Take last yarn end B through the center of the flower and through the block to tuck this end of the rib into the center of the flower.

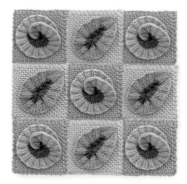

Mix and Match 40 + 41

41 BEGONIA LEAF
Beginner

Knit two, purl two rib suggests the veins on this pointed leaf, although it's not quite as simple as it looks, as some shaping is also used to give it definition. Like the Ribbed Rose (page 77), it sits on a corner-to-corner garter stitch block.

METHOD

Yarn Sport-weight wool in olive (A), leaf green (B), and sky blue (C)

Equipment A pair of knitting needles

LEAF
Using A and leaving a long end, cast on 32 sts.
1st row (RS) K2, [yo, p1, k2] 10 times. 42 sts.
2nd row P2, [k1, k1tbl, p2] 10 times.
Change to B.
3rd row K2, [p2, k2] 10 times.
4th row P2, yo, k2, yo, [p2, k2] twice, [p2, yo, k2, yo] 4 times, p2, [k2, p2] twice, yo, k2, yo, p2. 54 sts.
5th row K2, p1tbl, p2, p1tbl, [k2, p2] twice, k2, [p1tbl, p2, p1tbl, k2] 4 times, [p2, k2] twice, p1tbl, p2, p1tbl, k2.
6th row P2, k4, [p2, k2] twice, [k2, k4] 4 times, p2, [k2, p2] twice, k4, p2.

7th row K2, p4, [k2, p2] twice, [k2, p4] 4 times, k2, [p2, k2] twice, p4, k2.
8th row As 6th row.
Bind off in pattern.

BLOCK
Using C, cast on 2 sts.
1st row (RS) Kfb, k1. 3 sts.
2nd and WS rows K.
3rd row [Kfb] twice, k1. 5 sts.
5th row Kfb, k2, kfb, k1. 7 sts.
7th row Kfb, k4, kfb, k1. 9 sts.
9th row Kfb, k6, kfb, k1. 11 sts.
Continue to increase in this way on RS rows until there are 27 sts.
Next RS row K1, k2tog, k to last 3 sts, k2tog, k1.
Continue to decrease in this way on RS rows until 7 sts remain.
Next RS row K1, [k2tog, k1] twice. 5 sts.
Next RS row K1, sk2po, k1. 3 sts.
Next RS row Sk2po.
Fasten off remaining one st.

Making up Square up the block and press lightly. Using matching yarn, join the row ends of the ribbed leaf and, gathering slightly, join the two halves of the cast-on edge. Sew the leaf to the block, leaving the edges free.

42 MICHAELMAS DAISY
Intermediate

Looking almost more like crochet than knitting, this multi-petal flower is not difficult to make and could be interpreted in lots of other colorways or placed on a different style of block.

METHOD

Yarn DK wool in yellow (A), purple (B), and gray-blue (C)

Equipment A pair of knitting needles

FLOWER CENTER
Using A, cast on 5 sts by knitting-on method (see page 24).
1st row (WS) P.
2nd row K1, [m1, k1] 4 times. 9 sts.
3rd and 5th rows P.
4th row K1, [m1, k2] 4 times. 13 sts.
6th row K1, [yo, k1] 12 times. 25 sts.
Bind off knitwise.

FLOWER PETALS
1st row RS facing and using B, insert needle in first eyelet of 6th row, pick up and k one st, [yo, pick up and k one st in next eyelet] 11 times. 23 sts.
2nd row P.
3rd row K1, [yo, k1] 22 times. 45 sts.
Bind-off row * Cast on 2 sts, bind off 4 sts, slip remaining st back on to left-hand needle; repeat from *, ending bind off 5 sts.

BLOCK
Using C, cast on 32 sts by the thumb method (see page 24). Beginning with a k row, work 39 rows st-st, or until work is square (see page 32).
Bind off knitwise.

To neaten the sides, RS facing and using C, pick up and k23 sts along one edge then bind off knitwise. Do the same along the second edge.

Making up Gather the cast-on stitches in the flower center then seam the row ends. Center the flower on the block and, using B, backstitch in place between the B eyelets.

Mix and Match 42 (different colorways)

43 LILY
Intermediate

A combination of turning rows, shapings and welting gives a three-dimensional appearance to the petals of this naïve lily, without any padding. It sits on a corner-to-corner garter stitch block.

METHOD

Yarn DK wool in white (A), leaf green (B), sky blue (C), and yellow (D)

Equipment A pair of knitting needles and a wool needle

Note Each time a turn is made mid-row the wrap-and-turn technique should be used to prevent a hole: before turning, take the yarn to the opposite side of the work, slip the next st purlwise from the left-hand needle to the right-hand needle, return the yarn to the original side of the work, slip the st back on to the left-hand needle, turn, tension the yarn ready to work the next st.

FLOWER
Using A, cast on 14 sts.
Set-up row P.
Now pattern:
1st row (RS) P1, pfb, p9, turn, k9, kfb, k2. 16 sts.
2nd row (RS) P1, pfb, p8, turn, k8, kfb, k2. 18 sts.
3rd row (RS) Cast on 2 sts by cable method (see page 24), bind off 2 sts knitwise, p2tog, p6, turn, k5, k2tog, k1. 16 sts.
4th row (RS) P1, p2tog, p1, turn, k2tog, k1. 14 sts.

5th row (RS) K.
6th row (WS) Slip 1 purlwise, p13.
Repeat 1st–6th rows twice more, then work 1st–5th rows again.
Bind off knitwise.

STEM
RS facing and using A, pick up and k6 sts along st-st row ends, one and a half sts from edge. Change to B.
1st and 3rd rows P.
2nd row K.
4th row [K2tog] 3 times. 3 sts.
Beginning with a p row, work 17 rows st-st.
Bind off.

BLOCK
Using C, cast on 2 sts.
1st row (RS) Kfb, k1. 3 sts.
2nd and WS rows K.
3rd row [Kfb] twice, k1. 5 sts.
5th row Kfb, k2, kfb, k1. 7 sts.
7th row Kfb, k4, kfb, k1. 9 sts.
9th row Kfb, k6, kfb, k1. 11 sts.
Continue to increase in this way on RS rows until there are 31 sts.
Next RS row K1, k2tog, k to last 3 sts, k2tog, k1.
Continue to decrease in this way on RS rows until 7 sts remain.
Next RS row K1, [k2tog, k1] twice. 5 sts.

Next RS row K1, sk2po, k1. 3 sts.
Next RS row Sk2po.
Fasten off remaining one st.

Making up Using matching yarn and working underneath the stitches as far as possible, sew the stem and sides of the flower to the block. Catch down the tips of the petals and the inner points between.
Using D double, make 3 French knots (see page 30) on the block between the center petals.

44 FORGET ME NOT
Advanced

An unconventional mixture of crochet and knitting makes this three-dimensional flower, with its background radiating from the center in four sections.

METHOD

Yarn DK wool in sky blue (A) and lime green (B)

Equipment A pair of knitting needles and a crochet hook

FLOWER
Center
Using crochet hook and A, make 5ch, join with ss into a ring.
1st round (RS) 6ch, [1sc in ring, 5ch] 7 times, ss in first ch of 6ch. 8 ch loops.
Do not fasten off, do not turn.
Slip loop from hook and on to a knitting needle, the needle pointing left to right.
First petal
Cast on 5 sts by the cable method (see page 24). 6 sts.
* **1st row** (RS) K6, pick up and k one st from ch loop below. 7 sts. Turn.
2nd row K5, k2tog. 6 sts.
3rd row K6, pick up and k one st from same ch loop. 7 sts.
4th row As 2nd row.
5th row As 3rd row.
6th row As 2nd row.
7th row Bind off 5 sts knitwise. Do not turn, do not break yarn. **

Second petal
Pick up and k one st from next ch loop, slip 2nd st on needle over first st. Slip remaining st on to left-hand needle then cast on 5 sts as before. 6 sts.
Work as first petal from * to **.
Make 3rd, 4th, 5th, 6th, and 7th petals as 2nd petal.
Eighth petal
As 2nd petal to 6th row.
Bind off 6 sts knitwise.
Fasten off.
Join yarn end to base of first petal.
Pin out petals and press.
Turn flower to WS.

BLOCK
First quarter
Working into the front of the sc around the center ch ring and using B, [pick up and k one st in each of the 2 strands that form 1sc] twice. 4 sts. Turn.
1st row (RS) [Kfb] 3 times, k1. 7 sts.
2nd row P.
3rd row Kfb, k to last 2 sts, kfb, k1. 9 sts.
Repeat 2nd and 3rd rows 6 times more. 21 sts. P1 row.
Bind off knitwise.

Work 3 more quarters in this way, noting that in the ch that stands for the first sc it will be necessary to pick up one st in the ch and one st in the ch ring.

Making up Join the quarters with mattress stitch (see page 33), taking in half a stitch from each edge. Press.

45 POMPOM FLOWER
Intermediate

These flower petals are knitted in a strip and then joined, but what is interesting is that the fluted effect is created entirely by the shapings in the petals. A fluffy pompom completes the effect.

METHOD

Yarn DK wool in pink (A), turquoise (B), and pale yellow (C)

Equipment A pair of knitting needles

PETALS
Using A, cast on 4 sts by the knitting-on method (see page 24).
Set-up row P.
Now pattern:
1st row (RS) K1, yo, k3. 5 sts.
2nd row P3, p1tbl, p1.
3rd row [K1, yo] twice, k3. 7 sts.
4th row P3, [p1tbl, p1] twice.
5th row Cast on 2 sts, bind off 2 sts, k to end.
6th and 8th rows P.
7th row Ssk, k2tog, k3. 5 sts.
9th row Ssk, k3. 4 sts.
10th row P.
Repeat 1st–10th rows 7 times more.
Bind off.
Pin out petals and press. RS facing and using A, pick up and k one st in each alternate row end along straight edge. 41 sts.
1st row K.
2nd row K1, [k2tog] 20 times. 21 sts.
Break yarn and take thread through sts to lightly gather them. Join cast-on and bound-off edges.

BLOCK
Using B, cast on 29 sts.
1st row (RS) K1, [p1, k1] 14 times.
2nd row As 1st row. Repeat these 2 rows until 45 rows have been completed.
Bind off knitwise.
To neaten the sides, RS facing and using B, pick up and k29 sts along one edge then bind off knitwise. Do the same along the second edge.

Making up Arrange the fluted petals so that the seam is hidden in a fold, then catch down in the center of the block and by stitching underneath the tip of each petal. Using C, make a fairly full pompom, trim it, use the point of a needle to separate the strands of yarn to fluff it up, then sew it in the center of the flower.

Mix and Match 45 (different colorways)

46 FRAMED DAISY
Intermediate

A mixture of techniques are used in this naïve daisy, but it really isn't too difficult to make. The leaves curve thanks to increases and decreases, while the background color is stranded behind. The flower head is worked in intarsia to keep its roundness.

Stitch Key

☐ k on RS, p on WS

◿ k2tog

◺ skpo

U make a st by inserting left-hand needle under strand A between sts from front to back and k this tbl

B make bobble: (k1, p1, k1) in one st, turn, p3, turn, k3, pass 2nd and 3rd sts over first st

Color Key

■ A

■ B

☐ C

■ D

METHOD

Yarn DK wool in gray-blue (A), bright green (B), soft white (C), yellow (D), and pale green (E).

Equipment A pair of knitting needles

BLOCK

Using A, cast on 25 sts. Beginning with a k row, work in st-st from the chart, reading RS rows from right to left and WS rows from left to right, as indicated by the row numbering. Use a separate length of yarn for each leaf from 20th row onward.
When 34th row has been completed, bind off.

BORDER

RS facing and using E, pick up and k25 sts along cast-on edge.
1st row K.
2nd row Kfb, k to last 2 sts, kfb, k1. 27 sts.
Repeat 1st and 2nd rows once. 29 sts.
Bind off knitwise.
Edge remaining 3 sides to match.

Making up Join the mitered corners of the border.

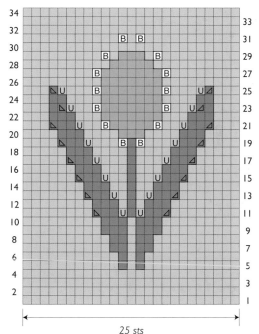

25 sts

47 POSY
Intermediate

The ribbed stems of this small posy are gathered in by a large cable. The flower heads are threesomes of small bobbles.

Stitch Key

☐ k on RS, p on WS

● p on RS, k on WS

⟋⟋ c3bp: slip 2 sts onto cable needle, hold at back, k1 then p2 from cable needle

⟍⟍• c3fp: slip one st onto cable needle, hold at front, p2 then k1 from cable needle

⟋⟋ c2bp: slip one st onto cable needle, hold at back, k1 then p1 from cable needle

⟍⟍• c2fp: slip one st onto cable needle, hold at front, p1 then k1 from cable needle

⟨⟩ slip 6 sts onto cable needle and hold at back, k1, p1, k1, then work 6 sts from cable needle: [p1, k1] 3 times.

B make bobble: (k1, yo, k1) in one st, turn, k3, turn, pass 2nd and 3rd sts over first st, k this st tbl

METHOD

Yarn DK wool

Equipment A pair of knitting needles and a cable needle

Cast on 23 sts by the thumb method (see page 24). Beginning with a p row, work in reverse st-st from the chart, reading RS rows from right to left and WS rows from left to right, as indicated by the row numbering. When 29th row has been completed, bind off knitwise.

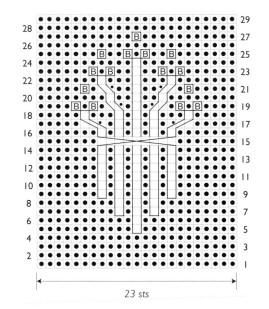

23 sts

48 BUTTON FLOWER
Beginner

Knit two, purl two rib forms the center of this rudimentary flower. It then fans out into a wider rib, suggesting simple, straight petals. A plain button is the finishing touch.

49 ZINNIA
Beginner

A perfect excuse to play with bright colors, the Zinnia is a length of eight shaped petals, joined into a ring. For piecing it can be treated as an octagon or as a round.

METHOD

Yarn Sport-weight wool in ocher (A), bright yellow (B), and teal (C)

Equipment A pair of knitting needles and one button.

FLOWER
Using A, cast on 42 sts.
1st row (RS) K2, [p2, k2] 10 times.
2nd row P2, [k2, p2] 10 times.
Change to B.
3rd row As 1st row.
4th row P2, [yo, k2, yo, p2] 10 times. 62 sts.
5th row K2, [p1tbl, p2, p1tbl, k2] 10 times.
6th row P2, [k4, p2] 10 times.
7th row K2, [p4, k2] 10 times.
8th row As 6th row.
Bind off in k2, p4 rib.

BLOCK
Using C, cast on 2 sts.
1st row (RS) Kfb, k1. 3 sts.
2nd and WS rows K.
3rd row [Kfb] twice, k1. 5 sts.
5th row Kfb, k2, kfb, k1. 7 sts.
7th row Kfb, k4, kfb, k1. 9 sts.
9th row Kfb, k6, kfb, k1. 11 sts.
Continue to increase in this way on RS rows until there are 27 sts.

Next RS row K1, k2tog, k to last 3 sts, k2tog, k1.
Continue to decrease in this way on RS rows until 7 sts remain.
Next RS row K1, [k2tog, k1] twice. 5 sts.
Next RS row K1, sk2po, k1. 3 sts.
Next RS row Sk2po.
Fasten off remaining one st.

Making up Square up the block and press lightly. Using yarn ends or matching yarn, lightly gather the cast-on edge of the flower and join the side edges, taking in one stitch from each edge. Place the flower on the block and sew button through the center of both.

METHOD

Yarn DK wool in lime (A), mauve (B), and orange (C)

Equipment A pair of knitting needles

Specific abbreviation
mb make bobble: (k1, yo, k1, yo, k1) in next st, pass 2nd, 3rd, 4th, and 5th sts over first st.

Using A, cast on 74 sts by the thumb method (see page 24).
1st row (RS) P.
Change to B.
2nd and 4th rows K2, [p7, k2] 8 times.
3rd row P2, [k7, p2] 8 times.
5th row P2, [k2, s2kpo, k2, p2] 8 times. 58 sts.
6th row K2, [p5, k2] 8 times.
7th row P2, [k1, s2kpo, k1, p2] 8 times. 42 sts.
8th row K2, [p3, k2] 8 times.
9th row P2, [s2kpo, p2] 8 times. 26 sts.
10th row K2tog, [p1, k2tog] 8 times. 17 sts.

Change to C.
11th row K.
12th row [K2tog, mb] 5 times, k2tog. 11 sts.
13th row P.
14th row K1, [k2tog] 5 times. 6 sts.
Break yarn and take it through remaining sts to gather them up.

Making up Using yarn ends or matching yarn, join row ends. Press lightly.

50 FLOWER BED
Intermediate

This stitch is a repeat pattern that's usually worked in two colors.
But varying the colors throughout makes a summery garden scene.
A scheme of slip stitches means that only one color is worked at a time.

METHOD

Yarn DK wool in pale gray (A),
4 shades of green (B), and 4
shades of mauve and pink (C)

Equipment A pair of knitting
needles

Specific abbreviation
mb make bobble: p3, turn, k3, turn,
p3tog, take yarn to back.

Note All slip stitches are slipped
purlwise.

Using A, cast on 33 sts.
1st and 3rd rows (RS) K.
2nd and 4th rows P.
Change to first shade B.
5th row K.
6th row K5, [wrapping yarn
3 times for each st k3, k7] twice,
wrapping yarn 3 times for each st
k3, k5.
Change to A.
7th row K1, [slip 1, k3, slip 3
dropping extra wraps, k3] 3 times,
slip 1, k1.
8th row P1, [wyif slip 1, p3, wyif
slip 3, p3] 3 times, wyif slip 1, p1.

9th row K5, [slip 3, k7] twice,
slip 3, k5.
10th row P5, [wyif slip 3, p7] twice,
wyif slip 3, p5.
11th row K3, [slip 2, drop next st
off needle to front, slip same 2 slip
sts back on to left-hand needle,
pick up and k dropped st without
twisting it, k3, drop next st off
needle to front, k2, pick up and k
dropped st without twisting it, k3]
3 times.
Change to first shade C.
12th row P1, wyif slip 2, * [(p1, k1,
p1) in next st, wyif slip 2] twice,
(p1, k1, p1) in next st, wyif slip 3;
repeat from * once, [(p1, k1, p1)
in next st, wyif slip 2] 3 times, p1.
13th row K1, slip 2, * mb, [slip 2,
mb] twice, slip 3; repeat from
* once, [mb, slip 2] 3 times, k1.
Change to A.
14th row P, working each bobble st
tbl. Repeat 3rd–14th rows 3 times
more, substituting shades B and C
each time. K1 row, p1 row, k1 row.
Bind off knitwise.

51 60'S FLOWER
Advanced

Completely circular, this stylized flower uses a mixture of techniques, all involving garter stitch. The center is shaped with turning rows outlined with a few rounds of circular knitting, the triangular petals are knitted on individually, and then the border is picked up and knitted in the round.

METHOD

Yarn Sport-weight wool in dull yellow (A), burnt orange (B), soft white (C), and mauve (D)

Equipment A pair of knitting needles and a circular needle or set of 5 double-pointed knitting needles

Note Each time a turn is made mid-row the wrap-and-turn technique should be used to prevent a hole: before turning, take the yarn to the opposite side of the work, slip the next st purlwise from the left-hand needle to the right-hand needle, return the yarn to the original side of the work, slip the st back on to the left-hand needle, turn, tension the yarn ready to work the next st.

CENTER
Using pair of needles and A, cast on 20 sts by the thumb method (see page 24).
1st row (RS) K16, turn, k16.
2nd row (RS) K12, turn, k12.
3rd row (RS) K8, turn, k8.
4th row (RS) K4, turn, k4.
5th row (RS) K all 20 sts.
6th row (WS) Slip 1 knitwise, k19.
Repeat 1st–6th rows 20 times more, then work 1st–4th rows again.

Bind off knitwise. Join cast-on and bound-off edges, taking in the back strand of the cast-on and the chain of the bind-off to create a g-st ridge.
Gather the center tightly by taking A through all the slip stitches.

BAND
RS facing, using circular needle or double-pointed needles and B, pick up and k one st between each g-st ridge around edge. 111 sts. Marking beginning of rounds (see page 27), work in rounds with RS facing.
1st round P.
2nd round Kfb, k5, [kfb, k7, kfb, k6] 7 times. 126 sts.
3rd round P.

PETALS
Change to pair of needles and C.
* **1st row** (RS) K next 9 sts, turn.
Continue on these sts only.
2nd, 4th, 6th, and 8th rows K.
3rd row K2tog, k5, k2tog. 7 sts.

5th row K2tog, k3, k2tog. 5 sts.
7th row K2tog, k1, k2tog. 3 sts.
9th row S2kpo.
Fasten off remaining one st, leaving an end for sewing. **
Repeat from * to ** 13 times.
14 petals.
Fasten off.

BORDER
RS facing, using circular needle or double-pointed needles and D, fold petals forward to pick up and k one st in back loop of each st of last round B, in this way picking up and knitting 9 sts from behind each petal. 126 sts.
Marking the beginning of rounds, continue in rounds with RS facing.

1st and 3rd rounds P.
2nd round K.
4th round [Kfb, k8] 14 times. 140 sts.
5th and 7th rounds P.
6th round K.
8th round [Kfb, k6] 20 times. 160 sts.
9th and 11th rounds P.
10th round K.
12th round [Kfb, k7] 20 times. 180 sts.
13th round P.
14th round K.
Turn to WS and bind off knitwise. Use yarn ends to sew the tip of each petal to the border.

52 HARVEST LEAF
Advanced

This is a heavily textured corner-to-corner block, with the veins of the stylized leaf being picked up and knitted afterward. This sounds complicated but it's actually quite easy with a little practice.

METHOD

Yarn DK wool

Equipment 2 pairs of knitting needles, one a size smaller than the other, and a wool needle

Note Single slip stitches on WS rows are slipped purlwise.

Using larger needles, cast on 65 sts.
1st row (RS) K30, ssk, k1, k2tog, k30. 63 sts.
2nd row K31, wyif slip 1, k31.
3rd row K to center 5 sts, ssk, k1, k2tog, k to end. 61 sts.
4th row K to center st, wyif slip 1, k to end. Repeat 3rd and 4th rows until 5 sts remain.
Next RS row Ssk, k1, k2tog. 3 sts.
Next row K1, wyif slip 1, k1.
Next row S2kpo.
Fasten off remaining one st.
First pair of veins
RS facing and with bound-off corner to top, using smaller size needles, in 3rd g-st ridge from bind-off: * insert needle in top loop of st immediately to left of center slip st, fold work along g-st ridge, pick up and k1 in this st. Pick up and k1 in top loop of each of next 2 sts, turn. Slipping the first st knitwise, bind off all 3 sts knitwise. **
Fasten off, leaving an end at least 6 times the length of the vein or long enough to repeat the pick-up, bind-off process.
Break the yarn, thread it on to a wool needle and take it underneath the center slip st. Swivel the block to start in the top loop of st immediately to opposite side of center and repeat from * to **.
Fasten off, leaving a short end, take this to WS and darn it in.
Second pair of veins
Miss one g-st ridge, in next ridge work as first pair of veins from * to ** but picking up 5 sts each side of center.

Continue to make pairs of veins every 2nd ridge and make each pair 2 sts longer than previous pair until 7 pairs have been completed (15 sts in veins of 7th pair). Repeat last pair 4 times more, then work one pair 2 sts shorter than the previous pair.

53 FALL LEAF
Intermediate

Lozenge-shaped blocks looking like textured leaves fit together to give a zigzag edge above and below, with the stems hanging free for more texture.

METHOD

Yarn Sport-weight wool in ocher (A) and rust (B)

Equipment A pair of knitting needles and a crochet hook

Using A, cast on 25 sts by the thumb method (see page 24).
* Change to B.
1st row (RS) K.
2nd row P.
3rd row K1, m1, k10, s2kpo, k10, m1, k1.
4th row P.
Change to A.
5th row K1, m1, k10, s2kpo, k10, m1, k1.
6th row K. **
Repeat from * to ** 3 times more, change to B, then work 1st and 2nd rows again.
Now decrease:
1st row (RS) K1, k2tog, k8, s2kpo, k8, skpo, k1. 21 sts.
2nd row P.
Change to A.
3rd row K9, s2kpo, k9. 19 sts.
4th row K.
Change to B.
5th row K.
6th row P.
7th row K1, k2tog, k5, s2kpo, k5, skpo, k1. 15 sts.
8th row P.
Change to A.
9th row K6, s2kpo, k6. 13 sts.

10th row K.
Change to B.
11th row K.
12th row P.
13th row K1, k2tog, k2, s2kpo, k2, skpo, k1. 9 sts.
14th row P.
Change to A.
15th row K3, s2kpo, k3. 7 sts.
16th row K.
Change to B.
17th row K.
18th row P.
19th row K2tog, s2kpo, skpo. 3 sts.
20th row P.
21st row S2kpo.
Fasten off remaining one st.

Stem and center vein
Using crochet hook and A, make 10ch, miss 1ch, ss in back strand of each of 9ch. Do not fasten off. RS of leaf facing, make 1ch in each of center sts B (see page 30).

54 TEASELS
Intermediate

The texture in this monochromatic design is a small amount of seed stitch that defines the heads of the teasels. The stems can be knitted or worked in duplicate stitch (see page 30) afterward.

Stitch Key

☐ k on RS, p on WS

⦿ p on RS, k on WS

Color Key

☐ A

■ B

■ C

39 sts

METHOD

Yarn DK wool in soft white (A), charcoal gray (B), silver gray (C), and dull red (D)

Equipment A pair of knitting needles

Using A, cast on 39 sts. Beginning with a k row, work in st-st from the chart, reading odd-numbered RS rows from right to left and even-numbered WS rows from left to right as indicated by row numbering. When 50th row has been completed, bind off.

BORDER

RS facing and using A, pick up and k39 sts along cast-on edge. Change to D.
1st row P.
2nd row Pfb, p to last 2 sts, pfb, p1. 41 sts.
3rd row P.
Bind off purlwise.
Work remaining edges to match. Join the mitered corners. Press carefully, avoiding seed stitch.

55 ANGELICA
Intermediate

Small, loose bobbles form the seed heads of this skeletal wintry wildflower. The monochrome design is outlined with color in garter stitch using purl rows instead of the usual knit rows.

Stitch Key

☐ k on RS, p on WS

Ⓑ make bobble: using B, (k1, yo, k1) in one st, turn, k3tog, turn, wyab and using A, k this st tbl

Ⓑ make bobble: using C, (k1, yo, k1) in one st, turn, k3tog, turn, wyab and using A, k this st tbl

Color Key

■ A

■ B

☐ C

39 sts

METHOD

Yarn DK wool in pale gray (A), charcoal gray (B), soft white (C), and dull red (D)

Equipment A pair of knitting needles

Using A, cast on 39 sts. Beginning with a k row, work in st-st from the chart, reading odd-numbered RS rows from right to left and even-numbered WS rows from left to right as indicated by row numbering. When 50th row has been completed, bind off.

BORDER
RS facing and using A, pick up and k39 sts along cast-on edge. Change to D.
1st row P.
2nd row Pfb, p to last 2 sts, pfb, p1. 41 sts.
3rd row P.
Bind off purlwise.
Work remaining edges to match. Join the mitered corners. Press carefully, avoiding bobbles.

PICTORIAL DESIGNS

56   FANTASY FLOWER
Beginner

Irregular rings of color can become a semi-abstract flower without much difficulty. In fact, the chart needn't be followed too closely.

Stitch Key

☐ k on RS, p on WS

Color Key

■ A

■ B

■ C

■ D

■ E

METHOD

Yarn DK wool in turquoise (A), aubergine (B), orange (C), claret (D), and lemon yellow (E)

Equipment A pair of knitting needles

Using A, cast on 25 sts by the thumb method (see page 24). Beginning with a k row, work in st-st from the chart, reading odd-numbered RS rows from right to left and even-numbered WS rows from left to right as indicated by row numbering on chart. When 31st row has been completed, bind off knitwise.

To neaten the sides, RS facing and using A, pick up and k25 sts along one edge then bind off knitwise. Do the same along the second edge.

25 sts

57 DREAM FLOWER
Beginner

This simple, semi-abstract flower could be given lots of color variations. It could also be used as the basis of other freely drawn designs in the same style.

Stitch Key

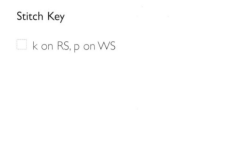 k on RS, p on WS

Color Key

■ A

■ B

■ C

■ D

METHOD

Yarn DK Wool in yellow (A), teal (B), crimson (C), and duck egg (D)

Equipment A pair of knitting needles

Using A, cast on 25 sts by the thumb method (see page 24). Beginning with a k row, work in st-st from the chart, reading odd-numbered RS rows from right to left and even-numbered WS rows from left to right as indicated by row numbering on chart. When 31st row has been completed, bind off knitwise.

To neaten the sides, RS facing and using A, pick up and k25 sts along one edge then bind off knitwise. Do the same along the second edge.

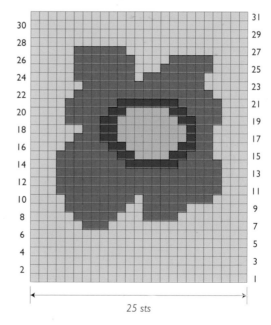

25 sts

58 PANSY
Beginner

Not quite symmetrical, there is something quite iconic about the flat, wide-open petals of a pansy. Its colors can be varied through all shades of purple and yellow.

Stitch Key

☐ k on RS, p on WS

☒ duplicate stitch

Color Key

◻ A   ■ D

■ B   ◻ E

■ C   ■ F

METHOD

Yarn DK wool in yellow-green (A), purple (B), deep purple (C), aubergine (D), acid yellow (E), and burnt orange (F)

Equipment A pair of knitting needles and a wool needle

Using A, cast on 25 sts by the thumb method (see page 24). Beginning with a k row, work in st-st from the chart, reading odd-numbered RS rows from right to left and even-numbered WS rows from left to right as indicated by row numbering on chart. When 31st row has been completed, bind off knitwise.

To neaten the sides, RS facing and using A, pick up and k25 sts along one edge then bind off knitwise. Do the same along the second edge.

Following the chart and key, use a wool needle and E and F to work the duplicate stitch detail (see page 30).

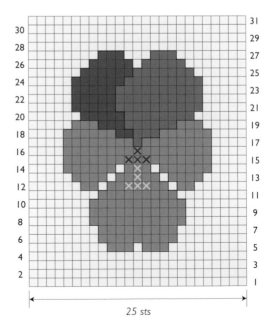

25 sts

59 TULIP
Beginner

A stylized tulip makes an easy-to-attempt piece of color knitting as it is completely symmetrical and the isolated spots of color are worked in duplicate stitch afterward.

Stitch Key

☐ k on RS, p on WS

✕ duplicate stitch

Color Key

■ A   ■ D

■ B   ■ E

■ C

METHOD

Yarn DK wool in violet (A), leaf green (B), gold (C), burnt orange (D), and yellow-green (E)

Equipment A pair of knitting needles and a wool needle

Using A, cast on 25 sts by the thumb method (see page 24). Beginning with a k row, work in st-st from the chart, reading odd-numbered RS rows from right to left and even-numbered WS rows from left to right as indicated by row numbering on chart. When 31st row has been completed, bind off knitwise.

To neaten the sides, RS facing and using A, pick up and k25 sts along one edge then bind off knitwise. Do the same along the second edge.

Following the chart and key, use wool needle and E to work the duplicate stitch detail (see page 30).

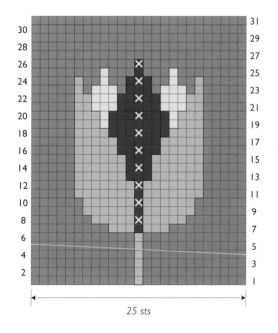

25 sts

60 MOCK ORANGE
Beginner

This is probably the simplest and most schematic of the intarsia flowers in this book. Made in other colors it would take on the appearance of another species entirely.

Stitch Key

☐ k on RS, p on WS

☒ duplicate stitch

Color Key

■ A

☐ B

■ C

■ D

METHOD

Yarn DK wool in sky blue (A), white (B), gold (C), and dark green (D)

Equipment A pair of knitting needles and a wool needle

Using A, cast on 25 sts by the thumb method (see page 24). Beginning with a k row, work in st-st from the chart, reading odd-numbered RS rows from right to left and even-numbered WS rows from left to right as indicated by row numbering on chart. When 31st row has been completed, bind off knitwise.

To neaten the sides, RS facing and using A, pick up and k25 sts along one edge then bind off knitwise. Do the same along the second edge.

Following the chart and key, use wool needle and D to work the duplicate stitch detail (see page 30).

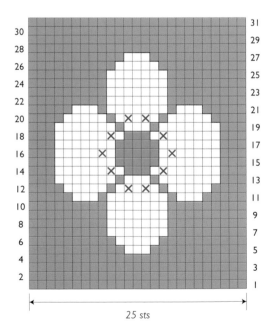

25 sts

SNOWDROP
Beginner

Here is a simple but unmistakeable flower that heralds the start of spring. It needs a dark background color to show it off, but this could be a deep blue to suggest a wintry setting.

Stitch Key

☐ k on RS, p on WS

Color Key

■ A

☐ B

■ C

☐ D

METHOD

Yarn DK wool in pea green (A), white (B), dark green (C), and pale green (D)

Equipment A pair of knitting needles

Using A, cast on 25 sts by the thumb method (see page 24). Beginning with a k row, work in st-st from the chart, reading odd-numbered RS rows from right to left and even-numbered WS rows from left to right as indicated by row numbering on chart. When 31st row has been completed, bind off knitwise. **Note** that the last row is entirely in A so that no contrast color is shown in the bind off.

To neaten the sides, RS facing and using A, pick up and k25 sts along one edge then bind off knitwise. Do the same along the second edge.

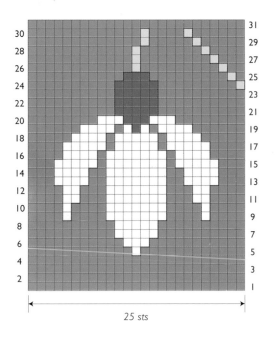

25 sts

62 THISTLE
Beginner

The regular, star-like formation of these petals is similar to the geometric flowers in Fair Isle knitting, although it is better to use the intarsia technique rather than stranding because of the number of stitches.

Stitch Key

☐ k on RS, p on WS

☒ duplicate stitch

Color Key

■ A

■ B

■ C

■ D

METHOD

Yarn DK wool in gray-blue (A), lime green (B), bright blue (C), and bright green (D)

Equipment A pair of knitting needles and a wool needle

Using A, cast on 25 sts by the thumb method (see page 24). Beginning with a k row, work in st-st from the chart, reading odd-numbered RS rows from right to left and even-numbered WS rows from left to right as indicated by row numbering on chart. When 31st row has been completed, bind off knitwise.

To neaten the sides, RS facing and using A, pick up and k25 sts along one edge then bind off knitwise. Do the same along the second edge.
Following the chart and key, use wool needle and D to work the duplicate stitch detail (see page 30).

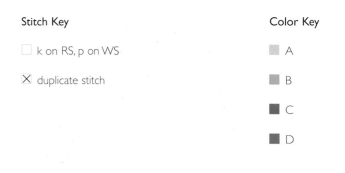

Mix and match 59 + 62

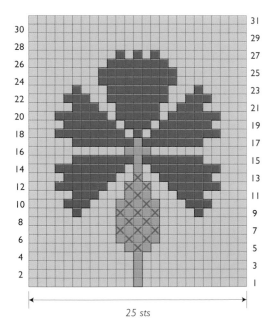

25 sts

63 FRITILLARY
Beginner

In the Fritillary, nature really does produce a regular checkerboard pattern that can be interpreted quite literally in knitting.

Stitch Key

 □ k on RS, p on WS

Color Key

■ A

■ B

■ C

■ D

METHOD

Yarn DK wool in leaf green (A), damson (B), dull pink (C), and dark green (D)

Equipment A pair of knitting needles

Using A, cast on 25 sts by the thumb method (see page 24). Beginning with a k row, work in st-st from the chart, reading odd-numbered RS rows from right to left and even-numbered WS rows from left to right as indicated by row numbering on chart. When 31st row has been completed, bind off knitwise.
Note The last row is entirely in A so that no contrast color is shown in the bind off.

To neaten the sides, RS facing and using A, pick up and k25 sts along one edge then bind off knitwise. Do the same along the second edge.

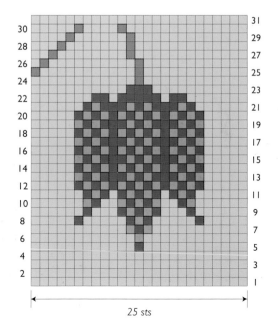

25 sts

64 ROSE BUD
Intermediate

This block could be used to punctuate non-pictorial squares or to accompany the more elaborate Rose design (page 101). Seed stitch, spotted or checkered squares would also be compatible with the Rose Bud.

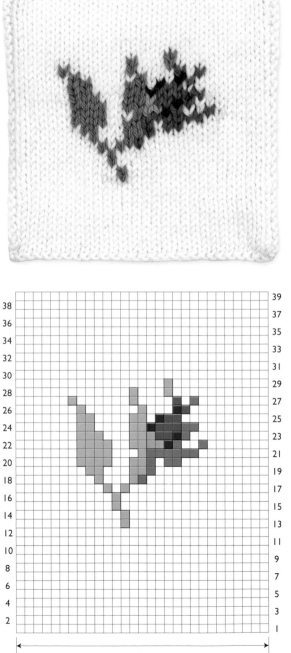

Stitch Key

☐ k on RS, p on WS

Color Key

☐ A

☐ B

☐ C

☐ D

☐ E

☐ F

METHOD

Yarn Sport-weight wool in white (A), mid green (B), dark green (C), pale pink (D), raspberry (E), and hot pink (F)

Equipment A pair of knitting needles

Using A, cast on 29 sts by the thumb method (see page 24). Beginning with a k row, work in st-st from the chart, reading odd-numbered RS rows from right to left and even-numbered WS rows from left to right as indicated by row numbering on chart. When 39th row has been completed, bind off knitwise.

To neaten the sides, RS facing and using A, pick up and k29 sts along one edge then bind off knitwise. Do the same along the second edge.

29 sts

65 ROSE
Advanced

A classic old-fashioned rose requires a lot of shades of pink and green and plenty of fiddly color changing for a high-definition result. But the effort is worth it.

Stitch Key

☐ k on RS, p on WS

✕ duplicate stitch

Color Key

☐ A   ■ E

■ B   ☐ F

■ C   ■ G

■ D

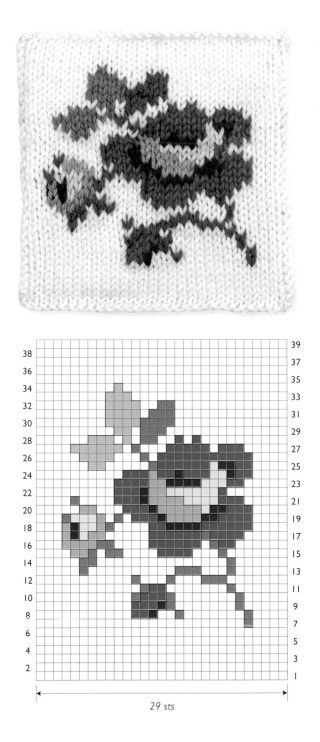

METHOD

Yarn Sport-weight wool in white (A), dark green (B), hot pink (C), raspberry (D), pale pink (E), faded pink (F), and mid green (G)

Equipment A pair of knitting needles

Using A, cast on 29 sts by the thumb method (see page 24). Beginning with a k row, work in st-st from the chart, reading odd-numbered RS rows from right to left and even-numbered WS rows from left to right as indicated by row numbering on chart. When 39th row has been completed, bind off knitwise.

To neaten the sides, RS facing and using A, pick up and k29 sts along one edge then bind off knitwise. Do the same along the second edge.

Mix and match 64 + 65

29 sts

66 FIG LEAF
Intermediate

Curvaceous fig leaves are very decorative and fun to draw and to knit.

Stitch Key

☐ k on RS, p on WS   ☒ duplicate stitch

⬤ p on RS, k on WS

Color Key

⬜ A   ⬛ C

⬛ B   ⬛ D

45 sts

METHOD

Yarn DK wool in pale green (A), bright green (B), dark green (C), and ocher (D)

Equipment A pair of knitting needles and a wool needle

Using A, cast on 45 sts.
1st row (RS) P1, [k1, p1] to end.
2nd row As 1st row.
Continue from 3rd row of the chart, reading odd-numbered RS rows from right to left and even-numbered WS rows from left to right as indicated by row numbering on chart.
When 56th row has been completed, bind off in pattern.
Following the chart and key, use wool needle and C and D to work the duplicate stitch detail (see page 30).

67 OAK LEAF
Intermediate

Although they're very recognizable, oak leaves vary considerably in their detail. This one has quite a frilly outline.

Stitch Key

☐ k on RS, p on WS ✕ duplicate stitch

● p on RS, k on WS

Color Key

A ■ C

■ B D

45 sts

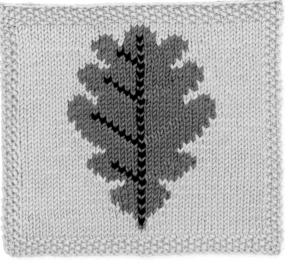

METHOD

Yarn DK wool in pale green (A), soft orange (B), rust (C), and pea green (D)

Equipment A pair of knitting needles and a wool needle

Using A, cast on 45 sts.
1st row (RS) P1, [k1, p1] to end.
2nd row As 1st row.
Continue from 3rd row of the chart, reading odd-numbered RS rows from right to left and even-numbered WS rows from left to right as indicated by row numbering on chart.
When 56th row has been completed, bind off in pattern.
Following the chart and key, use wool needle and C and D to work the duplicate stitch detail (see page 30).

68 ROWAN LEAF
Intermediate

Varying the colors within the Rowan Leaf suggests a season somewhere between summer and fall, but the colors could be made to suggest spring.

Stitch Key

☐ k on RS, p on WS   ☒ duplicate stitch

● p on RS, k on WS

Color Key

■ A   ■ C

■ B   ■ D

45 sts

METHOD

Yarn DK wool in olive (A), lime (B), soft orange (C), and rust (D)

Equipment A pair of knitting needles and a wool needle

Using A, cast on 45 sts.
1st row (RS) P1, [k1, p1] to end.
2nd row As 1st row.
Continue from 3rd row of the chart, reading odd-numbered RS rows from right to left and even-numbered WS rows from left to right as indicated by row numbering on chart.
When 56th row has been completed, bind off in pattern.
Following the chart and key, use wool needle and D to work the duplicate stitch detail (see page 30).

69 LIME LEAF
Beginner

The heart-shaped lime leaf has a classic outline and is relatively easy to knit.

Stitch Key

☐ k on RS, p on WS   ☒ duplicate stitch

● p on RS, k on WS

Color Key

☐ A   ■ C

■ B   ☐ D

45 sts

METHOD

Yarn DK wool in pale green (A), leaf green (B), dark green (C), and soft green (D)

Equipment A pair of knitting needles and a wool needle

Using A, cast on 45 sts.
1st row (RS) P1, [k1, p1] to end.
2nd row As 1st row.
Continue from 3rd row of the chart, reading odd-numbered RS rows from right to left and even-numbered WS rows from left to right as indicated by row numbering on chart.
When 56th row has been completed, bind off in pattern.
Following the chart and key, use wool needle and C and D to work the duplicate stitch detail (see page 30).

70 TULIP TREE LEAF
Beginner

Very elegant in outline, the tulip tree leaf is another shape that is relatively easy to knit.

Stitch Key

☐ k on RS, p on WS ☒ duplicate stitch

● p on RS, k on WS

Color Key

■ A   ■ C

■ B   ☐ D

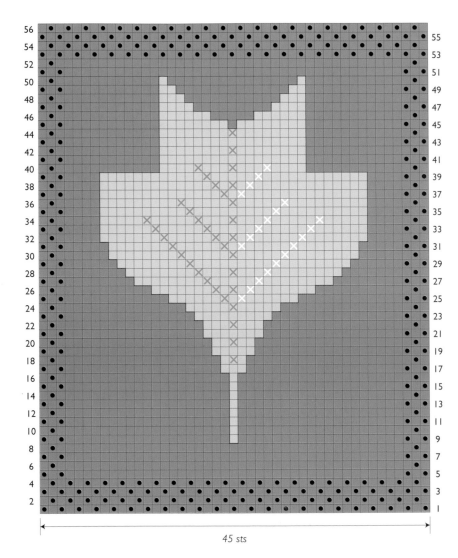

45 sts

METHOD

Yarn DK wool in olive (A), lime (B), bright green (C), and pale green (D)

Equipment A pair of knitting needles and a wool needle

Using A, cast on 45 sts.
1st row (RS) P1, [k1, p1] to end.
2nd row As 1st row.
Continue from 3rd row of the chart, reading odd-numbered RS rows from right to left and even-numbered WS rows from left to right as indicated by row numbering on chart.
When 56th has been completed, bind off in pattern.
Following the chart and key, use wool needle and C and D to work the duplicate stitch detail (see page 30).

71 CHEESE PLANT LEAF
Intermediate

Everyone must know the magnificent cheese plant with its lacy holes. This is the only one of the six leaf designs that isn't completely symmetrical at the center.

Stitch Key

☐ k on RS, p on WS   ✕ duplicate stitch

● p on RS, k on WS

Color Key

■ A   ■ C

■ B   ■ D

45 sts

METHOD

Yarn DK wool in leaf green (A), bright green (B), dark green (C), and blue-green (D)

Equipment A pair of knitting needles and a wool needle

Using A, cast on 45 sts.
1st row (RS) P1, [k1, p1] to end.
2nd row As 1st row.
Continue from 3rd row of the chart, reading odd-numbered RS rows from right to left and even-numbered WS rows from left to right as indicated by row numbering on chart.
When 56th row has been completed. bind off in pattern.
Following the chart and key, use wool needle and D to work the duplicate stitch detail (see page 30).

72 ORIENTAL POPPY
Advanced

The poppy is so distinctive that it's not necessary to show the petals in detail. Some of the center is in duplicate stitch for ease of working.

Stitch Key

☐ k on RS, p on WS

✕ duplicate stitch

Color Key

■ A   ☐ E

■ B   ■ F

■ C   ■ G

■ D

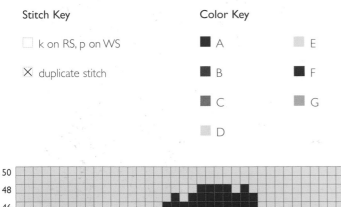

39 sts

METHOD

Yarn DK wool in scarlet (A), black (B), charcoal gray (C), gray-blue (D), apple green (E), maroon (F), and steel gray (G)

Equipment A pair of knitting needles and a wool needle

Using A, cast on 39 sts. Beginning with a k row, work in st-st from the chart, reading odd-numbered RS rows from right to left and even-numbered WS rows from left to right as indicated by row numbering on chart. When 50th row has been completed, bind off.

Following the chart and color key, use wool needle and G to work the duplicate stitch detail (see page 30).

BORDER
RS facing and using B, pick up and k39 sts along cast-on edge.
1st row K.
2nd row Kfb, k to last 2 sts, kfb, k1. 41 sts.
Bind off knitwise.
Work remaining edges to match.
Join the mitered corners.

73 | IRIS
Advanced

The delicate flaring petals of the iris require a large number of mauves and purples, so knitting yarn could be supplemented with embroidery wool.

Stitch Key

☐ k on RS, p on WS

✕ duplicate stitch

Color Key

▢ A	◼ E	◼ I
◼ B	◻ F	◼ J
◼ C	◼ G	
◼ D	◻ H	

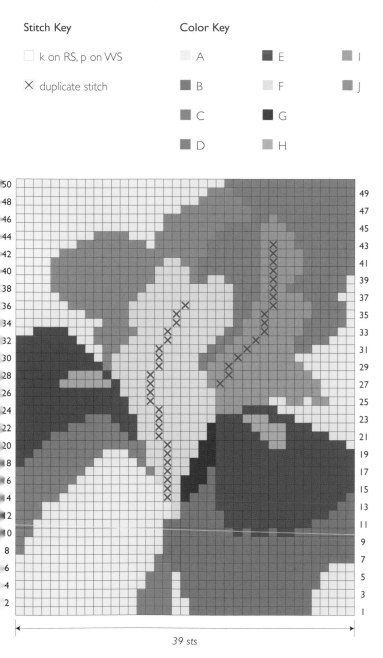

39 sts

METHOD

Yarn DK wool in pale lime (A), purple (B), dark green (C), pale mauve (D), deep purple (E), gray-mauve (F), violet (G), gold (H), heliotrope (I), blue-mauve (J), and black (K)

Equipment A pair of knitting needles and a wool needle

Using A, cast on 39 sts. Beginning with a k row, work in st-st from the chart, reading RS rows from right to left and WS rows from left to right as indicated by row numbering on chart.

When 50th row has been completed, bind off. Following the chart and key, use wool needle and J to work the duplicate stitch detail (see page 30).

BORDER
RS facing and using K, pick up and k39 sts along cast-on edge.
1st row K.
2nd row Kfb, k to last 2 sts, kfb, k1. 41 sts.
Bind off knitwise.
Work remaining edges to match.
Join the mitered corners.

74 AMARYLLIS
Advanced

The bold, trumpet-shaped flower of the Amaryllis is as uncompromising as its color. The stamens can be knitted in, as here, or added in duplicate stitch afterward.

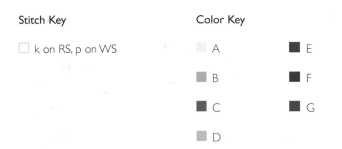

Stitch Key

☐ k on RS, p on WS

Color Key

■ A   ■ E

■ B   ■ F

■ C   ■ G

■ D

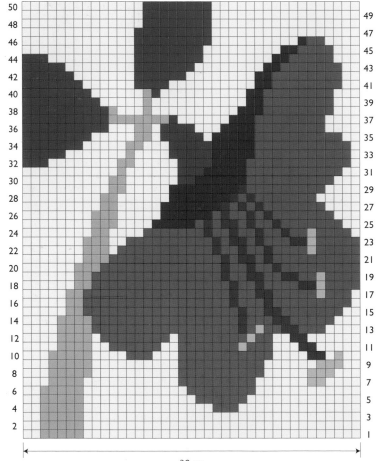

39 sts

METHOD

Yarn DK wool in lime green (A), leaf green (B), shocking pink (C), gold (D), maroon (E), crimson (F), fuchsia pink (G), and black (H)

Equipment A pair of knitting needles

Using A, cast on 39 sts. Beginning with a k row, work in st-st from the chart, reading RS rows from right to left and WS rows from left to right as indicated by row numbering on chart. When 50th row has been completed, bind off.

BORDER

RS facing and using H, pick up and k39 sts along cast-on edge.

1st row K.

2nd row Kfb, k to last 2 sts, kfb, k1. Bind off knitwise.

Work remaining edges to match. Join the mitered corners.

75 GERBERA
Advanced

The fresh, open face of a daisy-like flower is especially striking in strong, hot colors.

Stitch Key

☐ k on RS, p on WS

☒ duplicate stitch

Color Key

■ A ■ D ■ G

■ B ■ E ■ H

■ C ■ F

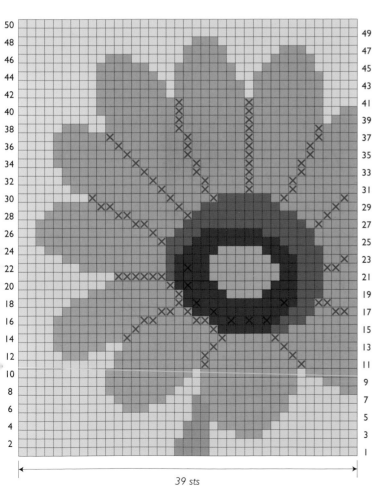

39 sts

METHOD

Yarn DK wool in leaf green (A), dark green (B), mauve-pink (C), shocking pink (D), orange-rust (E), gold (F), gray-mauve (G), crimson (H), and black (I)

Equipment A pair of knitting needles and a wool needle

Using A, cast on 39 sts. Beginning with a k row, work in st-st from the chart, reading RS rows from right to left and WS rows from left to right as indicated by row numbering on chart.
When 50th row has been completed, bind off.

Following the chart and key, use wool needle and G and H to work the duplicate stitch detail (see page 30).

BORDER
RS facing and using I, pick up and k39 sts along cast-on edge.
1st row K.
2nd row Kfb, k to last 2 sts, kfb, k1. 41 sts. Bind off knitwise.
Work remaining edges to match.
Join the mitered corners.

3
PROJECTS

The blocks in this book can be combined and used in a myriad of ways. This chapter presents a selection of stunning designs to inspire you with ideas of how to use the blocks in your own projects.

OPEN BLOOM HAT

Extending a traditional block knitted from the center, such as Open Bloom (page 39), makes a cute beanie hat. Additional rounds would make it a more ear-covering, pull-on design.

Materials One 50g ball Sublime extra-fine merino wool DK, a set of 5 double-pointed needles size 6 (4mm)
Gauge 22 sts to 4in (10cm)

METHOD
Follow instructions for Open Bloom (page 39) until 31st round has been completed.
K10 rounds straight.
Next round [K6, k2tog] 16 times. 112 sts.
K10 rounds straight. Bind off.
Gather cast-on stitches to make an additional bobble.

RETRO CUSHION

Enlarging a single block by knitting it in a suitably bulky yarn will make a small cushion. The 60's Flower (page 87) is round, but there are square blocks that could be given the same treatment.

Materials Debbie Bliss Rialto Aran in 50g balls: 1 ball in each of 4 colors, a pair of size 9 (5.5mm) knitting needles, 16in (40cm) felt, small amount of batting, sewing thread
Gauge 18 sts to 4in (10cm)
Size 13½in (34cm) diameter

METHOD
Using colors of choice, make 60s Flower block (page 87).

Making up Cut a circle of felt to fit block. RS facing and using sewing thread, backstitch block to felt along furrow between last round and bind off, leaving an opening for filling. Insert batting and complete seam.

BOUQUET GREETINGS CARD

Personalized greetings cards mean a lot and yet they can be very easy to make. The Bobble Bouquet (page 58) bursts out of a ready-made cut-out card from a craft shop.

Materials DK yarn as specified for Bobble Bouquet (page 58), a pair of size 6 (4mm) knitting needles, ready-made greetings card 5in (12.5cm) square with a circular window, 12in (30cm) narrow ribbon, double-sided adhesive tape **Gauge** 22 sts to 4in (10cm)

METHOD
Adding extra stitches and rows to background as necessary, make Bobble Bouquet block (page 58). This example was made using 25 sts and 33 rows.

Making up Press background, slot ribbon and tie in a bow. Use double-sided adhesive tape to attach block to card. Trim ribbon.

POPPY POT HOLDER

Bring a flower into the kitchen with a pot holder in a single, emphatic design. It would make a lovely gift, with the flower chosen to harmonize with a particular color scheme.

Materials DK wool as specified for Oriental Poppy (page 108) plus small amount more of black DK, a pair of size 6 (4mm) knitting needles, 10in (25cm) black felt, black sewing thread
Gauge 21 sts to 4in (10cm)
Size Approximately 7½in (19cm) square

METHOD

Make Oriental Poppy block (page 108).
Loop Using black, cast on 30 sts by thumb method (page 24). K1 row. Bind off knitwise.

Making up Cut felt to size of block. RS facing and using sewing thread, backstitch block to felt along pick-up rows of border and leaving an opening for loop. Insert ends of loop between block and felt, stitch securely then catch down edges of felt on WS.

PANSY KNITTING BAG

A patchwork of favorite flowers makes a dazzling front to an old-fashioned bag.
If this seems like too much pictorial work, make the front like the simpler
back (above) by including plain blocks.

Materials DK wool in various colors, a pair of size 6 (4mm) knitting needles, a pair of wooden handles (these could be home-made) approximately 11in (28cm) across, with an opening of 8in (21cm)

Gauge 21sts to 4in (10cm)

Size Bag approximately 13in (33cm) square

METHOD

Make 6 Pansy blocks (page 94), 4 Mock Orange blocks (page 96) and 8 plain blocks. Join 9 pictorial blocks for front, over-sewing them together as described on page 33. Centering remaining pictorial block among the plain blocks, join 9 blocks for back.

Facings Using any color and working into the chain of bind-off sts of top 3 blocks, pick up and k23 sts from each block and 2 sts from each seam. 73 sts. Beginning with a p row, work 29 rows st-st. Bind off. Work 2nd side to match.

Making up Press, then slot facings through handles, fold along edge of top 3 blocks and join bind-off edges to seams on WS. WS together, join base and sides as far as facings, over-sewing as described on page 33.

PHLOX BABY BLANKET

A bright spot of color in the center of each Phlox flower square
(page 49) punctuates this soft, deeply textured blanket. Each block
is knitted in the round, starting at the outside edge.

Materials Debbie Bliss Rialto DK in
50g balls: 9 balls of main color and
1 ball each of 5 contrast colors,
a pair of size 6 (4mm) knitting
needles and a size E (3.5mm)
crochet hook
Gauge 20sts to 4in (10cm)
Size Approximately 25in (64cm)
square

METHOD
Following the instructions for Phlox
Variation (page 49) and using a
contrast color for the center of
each set of 5 blocks, make
25 blocks.
Joining RS together, using crochet
hook and main color, join 5 blocks
into strips with sc as described on
page 33. Join these 5 strips in the
same way to form a square.
Edging RS facing and starting in a
corner, using size E (3.5mm) hook
and main color, * 3sc in corner, 1sc
in each edge st, 2dc in each seam
ending; repeat from * around
4 sides, join with ss, fasten off.
Using a contrast color, WS facing
and starting in a corner, * 2sc in
corner, 1sc in each edge st, join
with ss, fasten off.
Pressing Damp press all crochet,
lightly press reverse stockinette
stitch on knitted blocks.

LEAF BIRDCAGE COVER

Of course, not everyone needs a cover for a parrot cage, but this patchwork of leaves could be extended to make a throw of any size. Parrot lovers please note that Woodstock doesn't live in this cage, she's a free-range bird.

Materials DK yarn as specified in 6 leaf designs (pages 102–107), a pair of size 6 (4mm) knitting needles
Gauge Approximately 22 sts to 4in (10cm)
Size Approximately 24in (60cm) square

METHOD
Following instructions for leaf designs (pages 102–107), make 9 blocks. This cover contains all 6 leaves plus one more Lime, one more Tulip tree leaf and one more Rowan. The colors used for these leaves have been altered slightly.

Making up RS together and using the darker color of the adjoining blocks, backstitch the blocks in rows of three (see page 33).

INDEX

RESOURCES

Many of the yarns used in this book were supplied by:

Debbie Bliss and Sublime

Knitting Fever Inc.

315 Bayview Avenue

Amityville

NY 11701

www.knittingfever.com

DMC Creative World Ltd

10 Basin Drive, Suite 130

Kearny

NJ 07032

www.dmc-usa.com

CREDITS

The author would like to thank everyone who helped make this book,
Phil Wilkins and Nicki Dowey who took the photographs,
Susan Horan who checked my instructions and all at
Quarto who were so enthusiastic.